Centering Prayer *for* Everyone

Centering Prayer *for* Everyone

With Readings, Programs, and Instructions
for Home and Group Practice

by Lindsay Boyer

foreword by Gail Fitzpatrick-Hopler

CASCADE *Books* • Eugene, Oregon

CENTERING PRAYER FOR EVERYONE
With Readings, Programs, and Instructions for Home and Group Practice

Cascade Books
An Imprint of Wipf and Stock Publishers
199 W. 8th Ave., Suite 3
Eugene, OR 97401

www.wipfandstock.com

PAPERBACK ISBN: 978-1-5326-9680-0
HARDCOVER ISBN: 978-1-5326-9681-7
EBOOK ISBN: 978-1-5326-9682-4

Cataloguing-in-Publication data:

Names: Boyer, Lindsay, author. | Fitzpatrick-Hopler, Gail, foreword writer.

Title: Centering prayer for everyone : with readings, programs, and instructions for home and group practice / Lindsay Boyer.

Description: Eugene, OR: Cascade Books, 2020 | Includes bibliographical references.

Identifiers: ISBN 978-1-5326-9680-0 (paperback) | ISBN 978-1-5326-9681-7 (hardcover) | ISBN 978-1-5326-9682-4 (ebook)

Subjects: LCSH: Contemplation | Spiritual life—Christianity | Prayer—Christianity | Pastoral theology

Classification: BV5091.C7 B69 2020 (print) | BV5091.C7 (ebook)

Manufactured in the U.S.A. MARCH 17, 2020

This book is dedicated to all those who long for God,
searching in the silence for a mysterious presence,
perhaps without using the word "God."

Whatever your beliefs or doubts, you are welcome here.

Contents

Permissions

Thanks for permission to reprint excerpts from the following previously published works:

"Night Prayer" reprinted with permission from the Anglican Church in Aotearoa, New Zealand and Polynesia—Te Haahi Mihanare ki Aotearoa ki Niu Tireni, ki Nga Moutere o te Moana Nui a Kiwa, *A New Zealand Prayer Book—He Karakia Mihinare o Aotearoa* (San Francisco: Harper SanFrancisco, 1997), 184.

"The Prayer of Jesus" (a paraphrase of the Lord's Prayer) reprinted with permission from John Philip Newell, *Sounds of the Eternal: A Celtic Psalter* (San Antonio, TX: Material Media, 2012), 86.

"The Peace of Wild Things." Copyright ©1998 by Wendell Berry, from *The Selected Poems of Wendell Berry.* Reprinted by permission of Counterpoint Press.

"Go in and in." Reprinted with permission from Danna Faulds, *Go In and In: Poems from the Heart of Yoga* (Kearney NE: Morris, 2002), 2.

"Cover Me with the Night." From *An African Prayer Book* by Desmond Tutu, copyright ©1995 by Desmond Tutu. Used by permission of Doubleday, an imprint of the Knopf Doubleday Publishing Group, a division of Penguin Random House LLC. All rights reserved.

"Gott spricht zu jedem . . . /God speaks to each of us . . . ." From *Rilke's Book of Hours: Love Poems to God* by Rainer Maria Rilke, translated by Anita Barrows and Joanna Macy, translation copyright ©1996 by Anita Barrows and Joanna Macy. Used by permission of Riverhead, an imprint of Penguin Publishing Group, a division of Penguin Random House LLC. All rights reserved.

"Primary Wonder" by Denise Levertov, from *Sands of the Well*, copyright ©1994, 1995, 1996 by Denise Levertov. Reprinted by permission of New Directions Publishing Corp.

Psalms 13 [14 l.], 39 [8], 4 [12], 84 [10, used three times], 93 [8, used three times] from *A Book of Psalms: Selected and Adapted from the Hebrew* by Stephen Mitchell. Copyright © 1993 by Stephen Mitchell. Reprinted by permission of HarperCollins Publishers. Psalm 93 with one word changed by permission of the author.

"The Guest House" and a portion of "Be Melting Snow" reprinted with permission from Rumi, *The Essential Rumi,* translated by Coleman Barks with John Moyne (New York: HarperCollins, 1995), 13, 109.

Excerpts from Psalm 29 reprinted with permission from *The Saint Helena Psalter* (New York: Church Publishing, 2004), 39.

Scripture quotations unless otherwise noted are from *New Revised Standard Version Bible*, copyright © 1989 National Council of the Churches of Christ in the United States of America. All rights reserved worldwide. When the first referent to a person is a pronoun I have changed it to the person's name, e.g. Jesus, for clarity.

List of Essential Instructions in Boxes

Foreword

Let yourself be silently drawn
by the stronger pull of what you really love.

—Rumi[i]

In the early seventies I was called to silence, to go apart and carve out a place for silence in my life. At the time I had three children under the age of six and had no time for silence or time to be alone. I had a simple hunger to be with myself for more than an hour, and longed for a few days apart. I wasn't sure how to go about carving out this space for myself; I just knew it was important to me to do it. I didn't even know where to go. My beloved mother volunteered to take care of my children and I just got in the car and drove south to a small seaside village and looked for a place to stay. I wanted to be in the sun, on the beach, and listen to the waves rolling into shore, watch the seagulls floating on the air waves, and smell the salty air. I did not think of this time as searching for anything in particular, rather a time for absorbing my surrounds without conversation or company. I felt an inner longing and could not name it. I have since discovered it was a call to contemplative life outside the cloister. I was not familiar with the term "contemplation" and did not know that was what I was seeking. I was brought up in traditional Roman Catholicism which did not offer a pathway to contemplation.

After my "alone" stay at the beach I began to seek simple ways to be silent. My first encounter with silent practice was at a yoga class offered by the local high school. I took to it immediately and I began to practice weekly with the group. Afterwards I started my personal meditation practice and began to search for a community to practice with. This journey took me East to a Tibetan teacher who wisely pointed me in the direction of Christian contemplation. He said to me, "You are a Christian contemplative woman and you must find the way of Thomas Merton." I wasn't familiar with Merton at the time. I started reading his books and a world of contemplative life was quickly revealed to me. However, it was devoid of instructions or guidelines on how to practice Christian contemplation.

I was introduced to Thomas Keating and centering prayer in 1983. My eastern practice and what I understood about Christian contemplation came together and my daily practice and contemplative commitment was confirmed. From there I went on to support the work of Keating and centering prayer through Contemplative Outreach, a network of individuals and small faith communities that foster centering prayer and other contemplative practices.

I began my work in 1986 as Executive Director of Contemplative Outreach and later as President, retiring in 2016. During those years, I was one of the three founding members of CO and worked closely with Keating as an advisor, editor, and writer. We worked together to create, develop, and articulate the vision and principles of Contemplative Outreach; revised the centering prayer method and its brochure outlining the essential elements and details of centering prayer; created four filmed teaching series; developed and led silent retreats on each series; wrote books, resource guides, articles, training programs, and presentations; developed administrative resources; and offered spiritual guidance to contemplative practitioners worldwide.

Centering Prayer for Everyone is a little gem, a concise guide to contemplative practice offering all the tools needed to begin and sustain a practice of centering prayer and four other practices—lectio divina, visio divina, walking meditation, and chanting the Psalms, along with suggestions for home practice and information about the need for silent-practice-based community. This guidebook would have been such a support to me back in the seventies because it is brimming over with ways and means to practice silence: formats, beautiful prayers, resources, and everything you as a budding contemplative need to carve out and create a place for silence within your heart and within your own home. Simply said, you need a place to return to each day where you can renew your intention to consent to the Spirit within—it does not have be elaborate—a chair in a quiet corner of the room will suffice. Then follow the guidelines and suggestions in the chapter "Suggestions for Contemplative Home Practice," which will launch your home practice. Perhaps find a contemplative prayer group in your neighborhood and attend on a weekly, bi-weekly or monthly basis—here you will find others on the journey. Avail yourself of the resources outlined in Part IV and renew the essential instructions regularly. Pray for guidance, seek companions and most of all be kind and grateful—you can trust the stirrings of the Spirit within your heart. Keep in mind that every living thing is surrounded by God's awareness. Your intentions are already known. Most of all keep in mind the final results are not up to you—practice is just that: practice. It is not perfection, so relax and let go of expectations for achieving great goals.

Centering Prayer for Everyone is a treasure trove of information on how to participate in and lead a contemplative prayer group centered on silence, practice, and ritual for ordinary folk. More than an instructional guide to practice it is a companion on the contemplative journey. It provides a guide to silent prayer practice for everyone seeking a deeper relationship with the Spirit of God that dwells within. There is an intentional effort made herein to leave out non-inclusive language of institutional religion and rituals. This book makes a place for contemplatives who find themselves outside of traditional religious paths and yet have an interest in God and the teachings of Jesus. It is a guide to learning to speak God's first language—silence!

This book by Lindsay Boyer offers a pathway filled with helps for contemplatives to find their own way to silent practice and ultimately to God as they understand the notion of God. Here you will find support and guidance for your spiritual journey. Our prayer is that the Spirit will reveal to you what is most necessary for your growth in contemplative life.

—Gail Fitzpatrick-Hopler

Time spent in holy solitude can silence
the noisy world ever at work in our minds.

—Nan C. Merrill[ii]

Acknowledgments

ANGELS, POETS, AND SAINTS helped this book to come into being.

My deep gratitude to Contemplative Outreach, Thomas Keating, David Frenette, Gail Fitzpatrick-Hopler, Fr. Carl Arico, Steve Standiford, Marie Howard, and all those called to offer the gift of centering prayer and its silence. My dear friend, teacher, and colleague David Frenette generously said *yes* the moment I asked if I could assist him with his retreats and gave me room to experiment wildly, make mistakes, and find my voice as a teacher. I am so grateful for all that I have received through him. I come to these practices after studying the work of David and Thomas Keating for many years and in some cases am no longer sure where their words and images end and my own begin. I regret if I appear to have appropriated anything that is not mine.

Over many years of practice together, my steadfast fellow leaders of the Grace Church Brooklyn Heights contemplative prayer group, Jim Connell and David James, helped to bring this book and its programs to fruition with their prayerful companionship, inspired suggestions, and warm hospitality.

Gail Fitzpatrick-Hopler shared her vision of the seeker who might be longing for the practices in this book without knowing what she is longing for. With her luminous foreword and invaluable editing insights she has found many ways to help me invite that seeker in.

What a gift to have the timely and experienced guidance of my editor Dr. Robin Parry, who helped me navigate the maze of permissions, citations, and other complex matters of bringing my first book to print.

My thanks to Dr. Anne Silver, Director of the Center for Christian Spirituality at General Theological Seminary and the Queen of Group Guidelines, a dear friend who keeps inviting me into exciting projects that take my work deeper.

To the many who supported, guided, and inspired me along the way, including Betsy Roadman, Barbara Turk, Kathy Nelson, Liz Maxwell, Dallas Itzen, Kathy Bozzuti-Jones, Jane Sullivan, Carol Fryer, Ingrid Sletten, Mary Russell, Bill Adams, Judy Burns, John Philip Newell, the Rev. Canon Michael Hughes, Stephen Mitchell, Danna Faulds, Brandon Nappi, Miranda Chapman, Brian Chapman, Julie Shelton Snyder and the staff at The Gallery at W83, Paul Cooper, Sister Leslie of the Community of the Holy Spirit, Caitlin Stamm, K. Jeanne Person, Blair Burroughs, Carol Sanford, Win Sheffield, the contemplative prayer group at Grace Church Brooklyn Heights and all the Grace Church clergy and community members who have encouraged and supported me and the contemplative prayer group throughout the years.

To my spiritual directees and those who have attended the contemplative retreats, workshops, and groups I have led, my gratitude for your questions, your struggles, your tears, your longings, your insights, your ecstasy, your anger, your doubts, your determination, and your prayers. Our time together has been a blessing and an inspiration.

To James Martinelli and my dance companions, whose dance exuberance helped this book come bursting forth with an energy I wasn't expecting.

To my husband Mark, for his loving support of my practice, my writing, my time in silence and solitude, and my need to be a kind of monk in the world.

Introduction

Contemplative prayer is a way of saying *yes* to God's transformative presence. In contemplative practice, we create inner space in which to hear God's voice calling us into new ways of being and seeing.

This guide focuses on five contemplative prayer practices that use silence, spiritual reading, visual imagery, the body in movement, and the voice to draw the practitioner closer to God. Centering prayer is a form of silent, wordless meditation, similar to Zen meditation but which derives from the Christian tradition. Lectio divina is a way of listening to a reading with the ear of the heart, also from the Christian tradition. Lectio's visual cousin, visio divina, is a form of divine seeing in which we prayerfully invite God to speak to our hearts as we look at an image. In walking meditation, we move through space while remaining fully present, bringing meditation into action. Chanting the Psalms is a simple practice of singing prayers from Judeo-Christian scripture that derives from and is an important part of the Christian monastic tradition. These five practices complement each other and can very effectively be used together, as the programs in this book illustrate.

This book represents a particular approach to contemplative prayer, simple, inclusive, grounded in prayerful ritual and silence. By collecting in one volume everything needed to learn these five practices, including concise instructions, readings, and programs, it is meant to inspire beginners to enter the practices immediately and empower more experienced practitioners to start and facilitate groups.

The practices in this book come primarily from the Christian tradition, yet there are many people who are drawn to contemplative prayer who are not certain where they stand in relation to Christianity. This book uses inclusive language that welcomes everyone to these practices, whatever their beliefs. Many meditators who practice in Buddhist or mindfulness traditions that do not mention God nevertheless regularly experience the sacred in their meditation and these people are often very excited to discover in centering prayer a silent meditation practice that intentionally focuses on deepening relationship with God.

This is the book that I wish I'd had at the beginning of my faith journey. It describes the contemplative practices I've found most essential and compiles readings I've turned to again and again. It invites the reader into the contemplative world where you can be intimate with God even when your faith has no name.

My Faith Journey

I was raised an Episcopalian and attended seminary in my forties with the intention of becoming an Episcopal priest. When I realized I had a particular interest in those who have trouble making their way into churches, unsure where they belong, I let go of my plans for the priesthood and instead became a spiritual director. While I remain a Christian, I have learned an enormous amount about my faith by exploring the Buddhist and Hindu traditions. I am sensitive to the discomforts that many people have around Christianity and I try to find language that will invite people into contemplative prayer without setting off too many alarm bells. I present these practices in a spirit of openness that they may be used by anyone who feels drawn to them.

As a young person I longed to live by Jesus's commandment, "Love thy neighbor as thyself." But how could I become such a loving person? Listening to sermons and reading the Bible never seemed to bring me any closer. Christian dogma often sounded judgmental and exclusionary, and the history of the church suggested that Christianity might sometimes lead away from love rather than towards it.

Centering prayer derives from the Christian tradition and has its roots in Christian scripture and classic Christian texts like *The Cloud of Unknowing*, but as a silent form of meditation it can provide a method of prayer for anyone who would like to sit in silence with a divine presence, even if they are not quite sure what they believe. Most people are surprised to learn that Christianity has its own form of silent meditation. Centering prayer feels almost like a secret, and Christians who have turned to other traditions for silent meditation are sometimes a bit indignant to discover that such a helpful and spiritually nourishing practice is not more widely known. In centering prayer I seemed to find a piece that had been missing from Christianity. Jesus asks, "Why do you see the speck in your neighbor's eye when you don't notice the log in your own eye?" This practice began to teach me to see myself more clearly and honestly. Sitting in silence I felt myself being transformed by the sacred in ways I didn't yet understand and that sometimes startled me. At my first week-long silent retreat, I never spoke to most of my fellow retreatants, yet after meditating with them for a week I felt a closeness with them that made it clear that speech is not necessary to develop intimacy. When I had to leave the retreat before it was over, saying my good-byes in silence, my comrades and I touched each other's faces with gentle, eloquent gestures, like tender animals. I learned there that my quietness and introversion are not necessarily barriers to intimacy, that I have my own way of becoming close to people that does not always require chit-chat or a knowledge of someone's life story.

How This Book Came into Being

This book arose out of twelve years experience leading a contemplative prayer group at Grace Church Brooklyn Heights in Brooklyn, New York. Grace Church practices radical welcome as part of its mission and from the beginning we have tried to make our group welcoming and inclusive.

While some contemplative prayer groups take on a format that is somewhat like a class, with instruction and discussion, over time our group has developed into a simple worship service with a focus on silence. While a more conversational gathering can foster a more traditional sense of community, in our group we trust that silence and contemplative practice will connect us. Our regular participants and many of those who visit the group feel a sense of deep communion in the silence.

Several years ago two members of our group, Jim Connell and David James, stepped forward to co-facilitate with me and we began to rotate leadership on a weekly basis. It was at this point that I felt our group really come into its own. Jim suggested that we create a printed program to help newcomers follow along more easily, and this program with its similarities to and differences from that of a Sunday morning church service underlined the liturgical flavor of our group. As the three co-leaders selected readings for the group, we noticed that in spite of our different backgrounds we had shared tastes and a kind of canon developed of our favorite, most frequently used passages for lectio divina and chanting the Psalms. While I had begun the group in a traditional vein by using scripture passages for lectio divina, the practice of sacred reading, increasingly I have turned to poems and passages from the spiritual classics and other spiritual books and Jim and David join me in being drawn to a variety of types of spiritual readings. I began to use our printed program and canon of passages more and more as I visited other groups to teach centering prayer, lectio divina, and visio divina and realized that we had developed a template that might be useful to others.

Contemplative Prayer Is Real Prayer

Contemplative prayer is real prayer, based on Jesus's words in Matthew's Gospel, "Whenever you pray, go into your room and shut the door and pray to your Father who is in secret; and your Father who sees in secret will reward you." Praying in silence can be deeply transformative and fruitful, one of the most intimate ways to enter into relationship with God. The silence of contemplative prayer invites us to rest in the presence of God, where we may have a sense of having arrived home. There are people who long for God yet don't find what they're looking for in sermons and church services and in contemplative prayer finally arrive at their own true way to pray.

Worship based around contemplative prayer is real worship. Contemplative prayer does not necessarily need to be separate from regular church worship, off in the church basement. I hope this book will provide inspiration for those who would like to incorporate silence and contemplative prayer into worship and ritual. Why should this traditional way of praying, advocated by Jesus and practiced in monasteries for centuries, be consigned to the margins of the church? Because contemplative prayer has not historically been at the center of church life, we might have a sense that it is not proper prayer. As increasing numbers of people experience its transformational power, it is time for this to change.

The Episcopal church for centuries has used *The Book of Common Prayer* as the center of its worship. First published in 1549, *The Book of Common Prayer* contains morning and evening prayer services in numerous versions for a number of occasions; all the Psalms; and services for special occasions such as marriages and funerals. It is also commonly used for home worship. I grew up steeped in its rituals and when I describe *Centering Prayer for Everyone* to Episcopalian friends, it seems natural to them that I have created a kind of *Book of Common Prayer* for contemplatives. Yet many of my Episcopalian friends, including clergy, observe that the worship services in *The Book of Common Prayer* are extremely wordy, with almost no periods of silence. The programs in *Centering Prayer for Everyone* offer a respite from wordiness, dogma, and hierarchy, allowing for less mediation by a leader or clergy person and more direct prayer between the participant and God.

How to Use This Book

Please feel free to flip through this book and go straight to the chapters that attract you most. Perhaps there is one chapter that is very alive for you right now and the rest can be set aside for later. This book is designed to be as practical and accessible as possible and if you feel drawn to explore some of the practices, programs, or readings right away, don't let the other chapters hold you back.

Before exploring the contemplative practices described in Part I, it may be helpful to take a moment to think about why we might want to go to all the trouble of learning these practices and devoting our time to them. The chapter "Who Is God for You?" looks at how our ideas about God may help or hinder us in our practice and how important it is to spend a few moments at the beginning of our prayer time to connect with our sense of who God is for us right now. When we allow ourselves to feel our real feelings about God and admit how little we know about God's unknowable being, then our living sense of God's presence acts as a source of power, charging up our practice and our lives with motivation and energy.

Part I—A Concise Guide to Contemplative Practice

This section compiles the material that will be most helpful for newcomers to contemplative practice, providing concise instructions for centering prayer, lectio divina, visio divina, and chanting, which are deeply rooted in the Christian tradition, and for walking meditation, which is more closely associated with Buddhism. As a wordless practice, walking meditation can be used in any tradition to bring meditation into embodied action and provide a meditative way of stretching the body between periods of sitting meditation.

The chapter "Intuition and Following the Centering Prayer Guidelines" examines our sense of struggle in centering prayer practice and the way our practice may deepen into effortlessness as we develop a new relationship to the centering prayer guidelines and our thoughts.

"A Concise Guide to Chanting and the Psalms" examines not only how to chant a psalm in a simple manner but also why the Psalms are worth chanting. Full of poetry, joy, praise, and lament, the Psalms are rich with complicated and sometimes difficult God imagery that challenges us to go deeper in our understanding of God and the emotions we bring to our prayer.

While this book provides many resources for group practice, it can also be used by those who would like to practice contemplative prayer alone. A beginner might start by exploring a single practice and eventually add others. "Suggestions for Contemplative Home Practice" offers tips, including how to choose a place and time to meditate, how to set realistic goals, and how to avoid becoming discouraged. Those who are interested in a full prayer service for home use may consult the "Program for Contemplative Home Practice" in Part III and adapt it as appropriate. A contemplative practice is a home that can be carried anywhere, like the shell of a snail. The practices in this book can help you create sacred space wherever you go, connecting you with the community of all who pray, even when they are not in the room with you.

"The Need for Community" offers a brief examination of why community is important and how to find suitable, welcoming community that challenges and supports you.

Talking about prayer and the inner life is a new experience for many people and requires an attention to our speech similar to the kind of attention we bring to contemplative prayer. "Guidelines for Sharing in a Contemplative Group" examines the contemplative practice of speaking in a group and provides clear guidelines for spiritual discourse that can help us to honor the nature of what is being said as we talk about the inner life.

Part II—A Concise Guide to Contemplative Leadership

Many people feel that in order to be qualified to lead a contemplative prayer group they need to become an expert in the practices they will be leading. While experience can be beneficial, you can trust the silence itself to be the teacher. Experienced practitioners in the group may provide guidance and answer questions, yet the humility of the practitioners can be just as valuable. The longing for the divine felt by the participants in the group is holy and will do much to lead the group where it needs to go. The chapters "What Does It Mean to Be a Contemplative Leader?" and "Starting a Contemplative Prayer Group" offer encouragement to those who would like to lead a contemplative group. "Planning and Leading a Contemplative Quiet Day" provides inspiration and detailed, practical guidance for those who would like to offer a more extended period of contemplative experience.

I have offered centering prayer, lectio divina, visio divina, and chanting extensively in a video conference format, for which these practices are easily adapted. "Contemplative Prayer in a Digital Context" explores the advantages of this format for those who are having trouble finding a group nearby or who can't leave their homes easily. Even those who are technophobic and are able to attend a regular group may find this digital experience surprisingly moving if they give it a try.

Part III—Programs for Contemplative Prayer Services

If you are approaching this book with thoughts of beginning or enriching a contemplative group, the programs in this section provide easy-to-use templates that can be adapted in many ways. The "Program for a Regular Meeting," which in our experience lasts about an hour, is based on the one that has evolved over our twelve years of experience at Grace Church Brooklyn Heights. "Using the Contemplative Prayer Programs" outlines the details of this program plus three others, one incorporating visio divina, one designed for individual use at home, and one intended for digital groups. Perhaps these program formats are useful to you just as they are, or perhaps you prefer to use them as a point of departure for the group you envision. "Other Variations on the Program" offers outlines for a more talkative group, with time explicitly carved out for a discussion afterwards; a group incorporating an instructional video; a group integrating periods of music; and a program that might be used in the twelve-step tradition with centering prayer as an eleventh-step practice.

Part IV—Readings and Resources

Lectio divina is a traditional way of reading a passage of Judeo-Christian scripture with the ear of the heart. This book includes some traditional scripture passages for use in lectio divina. Once you experience the types and lengths of passages that work well it is not difficult to go to the Bible to find more passages that will suit you and your group. Other kinds of spiritual passages are provided in this volume as well. Even in a group in which all the members identify as Christian there are many ways of being faithful, and if you are trying to create a welcoming, inclusive space, other kinds of spiritual writing and voices may have something important to offer. As we draw closer to a God who grows ever fuller in our understanding and imagination, our faith can include our doubts and questions, our longing and our seeking, and passages from different contemplative perspectives and traditions can help to express the fullness of our faith. The ways in which scripture and other kinds of readings make us uncomfortable can help us to stretch and grow as we clarify what we believe.

There are many books that offer more extensive instruction in these practices. Some of these are listed and described in the "Resources" section. Your understanding of these practices can continue to deepen over a lifetime. Yet at the same time these practices are very simple and cannot really be done wrong. My hope is that these concise instructions and practical suggestions in one simple volume will encourage newcomers to plunge right in, referring to more detailed sources of instruction as needed. When seeking deeper relationship with God, there is no substitute for your own experience of prayer. You can trust that the presence of the sacred will be with you as you explore and open to these practices.

Who Is God for You?

Contemplative prayer is a way of saying *yes* to God, and before you begin it's useful to take a moment to be searching and honest about who God is for you and to whom you're saying *yes*. If you are filled with a mysterious longing to go deeper into silence through these practices, where is that longing leading you?

David Frenette, author of *The Path of Centering Prayer* and my own centering prayer teacher, emphasizes that taking time to renew our sense of who God is for us can help us maintain our sense of motivation and enthusiasm for our contemplative prayer practice. David quotes the great sixteenth century mystic Teresa of Avila, who wrote: "All difficulties in prayer can be traced to one cause: praying as if God were absent."[iii]

In my practice as a spiritual director, people sometimes say to me, "Of course I don't think of God as a man with a long white beard!" However as you go deeper in your understanding of God, you may discover that you actually do have conceptions about God that are outdated, unwelcome and in conflict with what you want to believe. When you admit these ideas to yourself, then it becomes easier to let go of them and grow more intimate with God. If your spiritual practice is going to be authentic and alive, it's important to remain in touch with your real experience of God, even when it leads more deeply into God's unknowable mystery.

I once worked with a man who told me that he wanted to "kill the guy on the throne." After much inner work he realized that a part of him was worshipping a kingly, judgmental father figure, and once he could see that, he was ready to let go of that image. A friend of mine who is a sponsor in the twelve step movement invites her sponsees to write down all the words they associate with God. Then she asks them to cross out the ones they don't really believe describe God accurately. They look together at the remaining list, now much shorter, and she says, "This is where we begin."

Who is God for you right now? Perhaps your sense of God has grown old, like the skin of a snake that needs to be shed, and you are called into a new way of being with God. What are you adding to your idea of God that doesn't belong there, from your childhood, from your own personality, from your own particular kind of woundedness? Is your image of God a stern taskmaster, an angry judge, an unjust ruler? Has your sense of God become so abstract that it's somewhat meaningless? Is God so mysterious to you that you've given up trying to understand and connect? Are you angry or disappointed with the ways that God seems to have failed you and the world? Do you long for God's presence but feel only absence? Perhaps your sense of God is full of a joy, gratitude, or awe so vast that it seems to transcend the traditional religious imagery you were brought up with.

All of these feelings can be brought into your prayer life. Don't pray to an image of God you no longer believe in. Spend a few moments getting in touch with what you *do* believe and feel about God. Open to the mystery of what God might be, more vast and capacious than your understanding.

Sometimes the most effective way to get in touch with God is by remembering. Can you remember a moment when you experienced the presence of the sacred, in a surprising way, in a vivid way, in a way that changed you? A moment in childhood, in nature, in church, listening to music, dancing, or looking at a beautiful painting? Can you remember the feeling of how intimate that moment was? Taste that moment and allow its precious quality to infuse your practice and your life.

At the beginning of a period of centering prayer in particular, it's important to take a few moments to reflect on who God is for you. Then gently let go of your thoughts and feelings as you begin the main centering prayer period. During the practice of centering prayer you will not think about these reflections but they will inform your sense of openness to transformation by a living God. The silence of the prayer can enfold and embrace all your thoughts and feelings about God. Through the simple, wordless practice of centering prayer, anything that is not needed will begin to fall away naturally, drawing you into a deep intimacy with a God beyond your understanding. You participate in that process not by thinking about it, but by resting in the silence. When you take a few moments before you begin to reconnect with what God means for you, you infuse your practice with a greater sense of meaning and intention and participate more fully with the sacred presence during the prayer time. Allow your sacred word or breath to be a *yes* to God's healing presence even as you accept that you cannot fully comprehend this presence.

Surrendering yourself fully in contemplative prayer requires a deep trust. Who are you surrendering to? If you are afraid that God is judgmental, angry, or uncaring, how can you let go and rest in God? Does your conception of God allow you to experience your own basic goodness? God created human beings and saw that we are good, yet most of us have trouble believing that we are loved. The Christian theologian Paul Tillich wrote, "You are accepted. You are accepted, accepted by that which is greater than you, and the name of which you do not know."[iv] If you take a moment at the beginning of the prayer time to feel that you are accepted by God, it may become easier to enter fully into the practice of resting intimately in God's presence.

Part I

A Concise Guide to Contemplative Practice

A Concise Guide to Centering Prayer

CENTERING PRAYER IS A WAY of resting silently in the presence of God. It is deeply rooted in the Christian contemplative tradition but can also be adopted by meditators from other traditions who regularly experience the sacred in their meditation and are looking for a silent meditation practice that intentionally focuses on deepening relationship with God.

We may think of prayer as thoughts or feelings expressed in words, but it is also possible to pray with a simplicity beyond words. Thomas Keating, one of the founders of centering prayer, wrote, "Silence is God's first language; everything else is a poor translation. In order to hear that language, we must learn to be still and to rest in God."[v] Many of us have a deep longing to be with God in silent intimacy. The method of centering prayer teaches us to rest in that longing.

Background

In the 1970s a group of Trappist monks noticed that young people were increasingly turning to eastern forms of meditation. The monks—Thomas Keating, William Meninger, and Basil Pennington—knew that there were contemplative prayer practices from the Christian tradition that might be of interest to the broader public that had at one time been used in monasteries but had largely fallen into disuse. They set out to recover these practices and make them more widely available, developing the simple method of centering prayer based on their knowledge of Christian spiritual classics like *The Cloud of Unknowing*, writings by the Desert Fathers and Mothers, Teresa of Avila, John of the Cross, Thomas Merton, and Christian scripture, in particular Jesus's saying in Matthew, "Whenever you pray, go into your room and shut the door and pray to your Father who is in secret; and your Father who sees in secret will reward you."

Instructions for Centering Prayer

The experience of centering prayer can be like entering a strange new realm. Don't be discouraged if it feels unfamiliar at first. Centering prayer is simple but not easy. As long as your intention is to be with God and let God act upon you, you can't do centering prayer wrong.

Below you will find a short set of instructions, followed by more detailed instructions. The most important step is to begin your practice. The more detailed instructions are there when you are ready for them, but don't put off practicing because you're concerned that you don't understand. You learn centering prayer by doing. You might find it helpful to read further, but information about centering prayer is no substitute for your own experience of and commitment to the practice.

Simple Centering Prayer Instructions

- Sit with your back straight. You can sit on a cushion or on a chair. Set a timer, if you have one. Two sessions of twenty minutes each day are recommended, but if that feels like too much at first, begin with five or ten minutes. Allow your body to relax. Begin to notice your breath flowing in and out at its natural speed.
- Choose a sacred word of one or two syllables as the symbol of your intention to be open to God's presence. Choose any short word with which you are comfortable

to remind you to be present to God. Examples of a sacred word: Yes, Silence, God, Jesus, Amen, Love, Peace, Mercy, Let Go. Sitting comfortably and with eyes closed, silently begin to repeat the sacred word.

- It is also possible to practice centering prayer with a sacred breath as the sacred symbol instead of a sacred word. When using the sacred breath, you do not hold your attention on the breath continuously but simply notice it, touching it gently with your attention, whenever you realize you've been engaged with thoughts.
- Whenever you notice that you have become engaged with your thoughts, gently disengage yourself and turn towards God's presence, silently sounding your sacred word or gently touching your breath with your attention if necessary.
- At the end of the prayer period, remain in silence with eyes closed for a couple of minutes. This is an important transition time for bringing the prayer into daily life.

Posture

Take the time at the beginning of the practice to make sure that you are in a comfortable, stable posture. Sit with your back straight but not stiff, on a chair or with your legs crossed. You can rest your hands on your thighs, hold them in your lap or place them in any comfortable, stable position. Centering prayer is usually practiced with the eyes closed, but if you prefer to leave them open, rest your eyes on the ground a few feet in front of you in a gentle, unfocused gaze. Scan your body and notice if there is any physical tension you could release with a deep breath, a wiggle, or a shake. What are you bringing with you from your day that you could gently let go of before you begin? Find a posture that is alert and attentive but not rigid. Check that you are comfortable but not so comfortable that you might fall asleep. Make any adjustments that are necessary to make sure that you will be able to remain comfortable for the whole time of the meditation.

Don't hurry this part. It's tempting to plop yourself down, set the timer and begin, but if you take the time to settle into your posture deliberately, as if you were doing a guided meditation for yourself, your prayer will be more grounded and you will be less likely to discover in the midst of the session that your jaw is clenched or that you have fallen asleep.

It's also helpful to spend a moment at the beginning of the prayer session connecting with who God is for you. This moment of intentional connection can help you stay motivated and remind you of why you are taking the time to pray. The chapter "Who Is God for You?" explores this step in greater detail.

Think of the beginning and end of the centering prayer time as a pair of bookends. The main prayer period, what we usually think of when we think of centering prayer, is the heart of the practice, but each end offers vital support. The time you spend at the beginning and end of your session is brief but essential to helping your practice remain grounded, motivated, and fruitful.

The Sacred Word

Choose a sacred word of one or two syllables as the symbol of your intention to open yourself to God's presence. During the centering prayer period, silently and gently say your sacred word to yourself whenever you notice that you are thinking about your thoughts or engaged in interior dialogue. The sacred word points back towards God's presence and expresses your *yes* to God's transformational power.

You do not need repeat the word continuously like a mantra or use it every time you notice yourself having a thought, only when you are engaged and distracted by the thought. Pick a word that is very short and neutral rather than charged with emotion so that you will not be drawn into thinking about the word during the prayer period. It's best not to change the word during the prayer period.

Remember that there isn't a better word or a more sacred word. The sacred word is not inherently sacred but is made sacred by the way that you use it. Your sacred word does not need to be a religious word but can be any word that helps point you back towards your sense of the sacred, your own basic goodness, and the goodness of God.

When you are ready, you can let go of the sacred word and simply rest in God's presence. However, don't be discouraged if you need to return many times to your sacred word. Each use of the sacred word is an act of prayer.

Examples of a sacred word: Yes, Silence, Stillness, Faith, Trust, Holy, Glory, God, Jesus, Abba, Father, Mother, Mary, Amen, Love, Listen, Peace, Mercy, Let Go.

The Sacred Breath

Centering prayer is usually taught with a sacred word. However, in his seminal book *Open Mind, Open Heart,* Thomas Keating writes that it is possible to use the breath as a sacred symbol instead of a word:

> Noticing one's breathing can also serve as a sacred symbol of one's consent to God's presence and action within. In this case, one does not follow one's breathing physically as is done in Eastern forms of meditation, but simply observes it.[vi]

When you are engaged with your thoughts, simply notice the breath. Touch it very gently with your attention, without following it or changing it in any way. You don't need to get engaged with the breath any more than with your thoughts. Whereas in other forms of meditation you are sometimes asked to concentrate on each breath, in centering prayer you lightly touch the sacred breath with your attention only when necessary.

Some people are drawn to the use of the sacred breath at certain ages or stages of the spiritual journey. Sometimes people who have been using the sacred word for a while find that the word falls away and the breath naturally and spontaneously becomes their sacred symbol. These people may have a nagging feeling that they're doing centering prayer wrong, and it can be helpful for them to be affirmed and instructed in their use of the sacred breath.

The use of the sacred breath is not better or more advanced than the use of the sacred word. It's merely an alternative. The use of the sacred breath can be simple, grounding, natural, and relaxed, especially for those who have been practicing it for a while. For some people the sacred word may feel a bit harsh or encourage excessive thinking, while for others the sacred word feels more natural and anchoring than the sacred breath. The use of the sacred breath is a receptive, embodied practice that can open you to your felt experience. Like your thoughts, which never go away entirely, your breath is always with you, and it is simple to gently transfer your attention from your thoughts to your breath.

Relating to Thoughts

When you notice that you have become engaged with your thoughts, gently disengage yourself and turn towards God's presence, using the sacred symbol if necessary. Thoughts in centering prayer include body sensations, feelings, images, memories, plans, reflections, concepts, commentaries, and spiritual experiences.

Thoughts are inevitable, integral, and normal. If you didn't have thoughts, you'd be dead. You're not trying to get rid of them, you're gently disentangling yourself from them and making a bit more space between you and them. In centering prayer you are invited to become more separate from your thoughts, more aware that your thoughts are not *you*. They continue to flow by without interrupting your prayer unless you allow yourself to engage them. Let them come and go without becoming absorbed by them.

It's a common misconception that in centering prayer you are supposed to eliminate all thoughts, and often people will become frustrated and discouraged when they notice their minds wandering. When you accept that thoughts are not only inevitable but also a natural part of the process of healing and transformation, it becomes easier to take a friendly attitude towards them. In a story told by Cynthia Bourgeault in *Centering Prayer and Inner Awakening,* a student of centering prayer says, "Oh, Father Thomas, I'm such a failure at this prayer. In twenty minutes, I've had ten thousand thoughts." "How lovely!" responded Thomas Keating without missing a beat. "Ten thousand opportunities to return to God!"[vii] If you consider each moment that you notice you have been thinking as a moment of grace and an opportunity for prayer, then it's not necessary to judge the period of prayer as "good" or "bad." Let go of expectations such as feeling peaceful or having a spiritual experience and just be present to whatever is actually arising. God is able to use whatever happens during the prayer period towards healing in ways you don't have to analyze or understand.

Notice the quality of the way in which you use the sacred symbol. Are you making a tiny mental movement of tamping down or cutting off your thoughts? Is there an element of frustration, hostility, or aggression in your use of your sacred symbol that you could let go of? The sacred symbol is not a cork, a battering ram, or a knife. Use it gently as a pointer towards the sacred, then let it go. Remain in an open state, ready to embrace whatever comes to you in your prayer, and equally ready to let it go again.

Imagine that you are training a small puppy. You understand that it will take many tries to teach her to sit and stay. She will get up again and again and you will gently reposition her. You know that it will not be helpful to shout at her. That would just scare her and waste your energy. Similarly, as you train yourself to become less engaged with your thoughts, this strange new activity will require many, many, many gentle, patient attempts.

In centering prayer both thoughts and silence have an important role to play. Some thoughts contain what most needs to be healed in us. Without thinking about it during the prayer period and without needing to analyze or understand what is happening, we offer ourselves up to a mysterious process that Thomas Keating calls the divine therapy in which our emotional wounds are released and healed. Thoughts, silence, and our intention to surrender to the sacred all contribute to this healing process.

Transitioning Back into Daily Life

At the end of the prayer period, remain in silence with eyes closed for a couple of minutes. This is an important transition time for bringing the prayer into daily life.

If you feel unsure whether the fruits of the prayer are coming forth in your life, then you may be neglecting this often overlooked step. In the midst of a busy day, it's tempting the moment the timer goes off to leap up and start rushing around. If you take a couple of minutes at the end of the session to transition gently back into your ordinary way of being, you may notice that you are more likely to bring your prayerful practice with you into your life.

David Frenette offers five suggestions of ways to spend this time at the end of the prayer period:[viii]

- Let go of the practice and just rest in God, letting go of all effort. You've been letting go of thoughts, now let go of everything and rest completely. As you rest, you may become aware that during the prayer you were making more effort than was necessary. Ideally, in centering prayer you let go of your thoughts so gently that the practice is effortless. Taste this effortlessness now.
- Spend a few moments gently bringing your attention to your sense perceptions, your body, and your breath. You may feel that you haven't really been doing anything special during the centering prayer yet as you transition from the more wordless experience of your practice into your ordinary way of thinking you may notice that there is a big difference between the two. Notice if there are physical aspects of the centering prayer experience that you would like to bring with you and prepare to be more attentive to your senses during the day.
- Spend a few moments offering the period of centering prayer to a particular person or concern. Shift your focus from your inner life back into the world and its needs. Sense your connection with others and allow their needs to float up into your consciousness and become part of your prayer.

- Visualize yourself in an activity in your daily life, perhaps a challenge you are preparing to face, and imagine yourself bringing the prayer back with you into your life.
- Quietly say or read the Lord's Prayer, the Serenity Prayer, or another verbal prayer to make the transition.

Choose one of these approaches or find your own way to bring the silence of the prayer with you into your daily life. Some of the gifts of the practice that you may notice include a growing capacity to listen to others and to your own intuition; a less judgmental attitude towards yourself and others; an increased ability to see yourself clearly, for better or for worse; and an ability to let go of what is not needed.

Learning to Trust the Practice

You might feel afraid you're not doing centering prayer right. What is it supposed to feel like? It may not feel like you're doing much of anything at all. Anthony of the Desert, one of the earliest Christian monastics, wrote, "The prayer of the monk is not perfect until he no longer realizes himself or the fact that he is praying." David Frenette unpacks this rather mysterious statement of Anthony's in the following manner:

> Not realizing that *you* are praying means that *God* is praying, awakening, in you. Not knowing that you are praying means that the workings of your intellectual mind are unknown or secret from your awareness and from the self who lives behind reflective thinking. Anthony's perfect form of prayer—pure contemplation—shifts you away from having your identity defined by your thoughts and thinking.[ix]

When you surrender to God's transformational movement, you let go of your usual ways of thinking and defining yourself through your thoughts and allow yourself to be acted upon. It's not surprising that this way of saying *yes* to God should feel very unfamiliar and mysterious at first. As you proceed, you can grow to trust what is arising through this silent process. Trust that you will receive what you need through God's action in your practice. Trust that the sacred is present with you, even if you cannot feel that or know what it means.

The Four Basic Guidelines of Centering Prayer

Let's close with the four basic guidelines, the most essential instructions for centering prayer. I think of them as a tiny suitcase that may at first seem too small to contain everything you need for your trip, yet it does. Whenever you feel unsure about how to practice centering prayer, you can return to these four basic guidelines, read them carefully, and unpack more of their concentrated riches.

The Four Basic Guidelines of Centering Prayer

1. Choose a sacred word or a sacred breath as the symbol of your intention to consent to God's presence and action within.
2. Sitting comfortably and with eyes closed, settle briefly and silently introduce the sacred word or sacred breath as the symbol of your consent to God's presence and action within.
3. When engaged with your thoughts, return ever-so-gently to the sacred word or breath.
4. At the end of the prayer period, remain in silence with eyes closed for a couple of minutes.

Intuition and Following the Centering Prayer Guidelines

Following the instructions will help you to go more deeply in your centering prayer. It's tempting to improvise or become distracted, particularly if you arrive at the practice with an expectation that you will have a spiritual experience or feel peaceful during the practice time. Those who come to centering prayer after years of experimenting with other forms of meditation may have a tendency to create a synthesis of more than one practice. For a certain period during my years of exploration I practiced a hybrid of centering prayer and Zen meditation until I realized that I was confused about exactly what I was doing. There is great value in picking a single practice and sticking to it with clarity and faithfulness. It doesn't have to be the perfect practice. Centering prayer provides a simple tool for learning to let go and become receptive to the sacred. The word "practice" makes clear that patient discipline is required and that the valuable fruits of your practice won't ripen overnight.

That being said, centering prayer is taught with guidelines, not rules. You may experience the guidelines *as* rules, bridling against the structures that are meant to help you, struggling with your relationship with authority even as it takes this inner form. Contemplative practice offers you an opportunity to become more familiar with the ways in which you may judge and oppress yourself in response to instructions. Your inner rebel may have difficulty committing to the guidelines and experience them as rigid or harsh. As you work as much as possible within the framework of the guidelines, you can trust that eventually and paradoxically they will teach you an inner freedom.

There are moments in centering prayer when you may become overwhelmed by an emotion to the point that you find it impossible to return to your sacred symbol. At these moments the instruction is to let the emotion become your sacred symbol and be fully present to the emotion until it disperses, as it always does, and you can go back to your regular practice. If spiritual experiences such as visions or profound insights arise during the practice time, the instruction is to let go of them, trusting that if they are genuinely important they can be explored when the period of centering prayer is over. While this is usually appropriate, there may occasionally be moments when something arises that demands your attention with a spiritual authority you can't ignore. Your faithful practice will teach you when to listen and when to let go. Trust your intuition and let the Holy Spirit be your guide.

When you begin centering prayer and find that you are not immediately able to fully understand much less carry out the guidelines, you are likely to feel a sense of struggle and self-judgment. Many people think that doing centering prayer "right" means not having any thoughts and making the mind a blank. This is not the goal nor is it even possible. In an effort to achieve this unrealistic and undesirable goal you may bring more struggle and effort into your practice than is necessary.

It's possible to rest effortlessly in the practice. When you notice that you have become engaged with your thoughts, you can return to the sacred symbol with great gentleness, almost as if you aren't doing anything at all but instead are receiving something from God. An unfamiliar inner movement of letting go and inwardly turning towards God begins to replace the more familiar movement of correcting yourself and feeling you've made a mistake. This unfamiliar movement develops its own momentum as you let go of your own doing, which tends to keep you trapped in the realm of "doing it right" and "making mistakes," and are gently led into the more mysterious realm of being able to rest effortlessly in God's presence.

As your practice deepens you may start to feel a growing sense of God's presence that enables you to rest in the practice and accept yourself as you are, allowing all of your thoughts and emotions to be present. The guidelines for the practice continue to guide you, and your growing intuition of what God is asking from you enables you to let go of what is not needed. When you say *yes* to God's transformative presence through this practice, you can trust in what is arising, even if you don't always understand it.

A Concise Guide to Lectio Divina

Lectio divina is an ancient practice of listening to a brief reading with the ear of the heart. It is traditionally practiced with Christian scripture, but it can also be used to access the wisdom of other spiritual writings. Lectio divina is not the same as centering prayer. It is a separate practice that can be especially powerful after a period of centering prayer. Lectio divina is not the same as Bible study. In lectio divina you let go of more intellectual, studious, or effortful ways of reading and enter a state in which you are quiet and receptive to God's voice. You let go of your own words and let God speak to you. In this contemplative practice, the words of the reading come alive and touch your heart in spontaneous ways that lead you more deeply into relationship with God.

Lectio divina has traditionally been practiced in a number of formal ways which involve the use of different steps. The steps can be helpful in learning how to be drawn more deeply into the practice, but it is not necessary to practice in such a formal way, particularly if you have just been practicing centering prayer or another meditative practice that has helped you enter into a quiet and receptive state, ready to allow God to speak out of the silence.

Lectio divina can be practiced individually or in groups. In some of the formats described below participants are invited to speak but no one is required to do so.

Instructions for Simple Lectio Divina

The simple form of lectio divina that we currently use in our weekly group is extremely accessible to anyone, even if they are visiting the group for the first time and do not have any opportunity for instruction.

The leader reads a passage slowly three times, leaving two or three minutes of silence between each reading. Participants are invited to listen to the passage with the ear of the heart, without becoming distracted by intellectual types of questions about the passage. Listen to what the passage is saying to you, right now. Notice if any phrase, sentence, or word stands out and gently begin to repeat it silently to yourself, allowing it to touch you deeply. After the final reading you are invited to share a word or phrase from the passage that resonated for you.

Instructions for Traditional Lectio Divina

Lectio divina is traditionally done in four movements, but these movements do not need to take place in any particular order, and you do not need to do each step. Even if you choose to practice the simple version above for your group or individual practice, it may enrich your practice to be aware of these four traditional movements.

Read a passage slowly four times, sitting in silence for two or three minutes in between each reading. Notice what is arising within you and be open to your own inner movement. Listen to the passage with the ear of the heart, without becoming distracted by intellectual types of questions about the passage. Listen to what the passage is saying to you, right now. During each reading, listen with a slightly different focus:

First reading: **Listen** with the ear of the heart. Notice if any phrase, sentence, or word stands out and gently begin to repeat it silently to yourself, allowing it to touch you deeply.

Second reading: **Reflect** while you listen to the passage again with deep receptivity. Notice what thoughts, feelings, and reflections arise within you. Let the words resound in your heart. What might God be asking of you through the passage?

Third reading: **Respond** spontaneously as you listen. Notice any prayerful response that arises within you, for example, a small prayer of gratitude or praise.

Fourth reading: **Rest** in God's presence beyond thoughts or reflections. Just be.

The resting in God that takes place in the fourth movement of lectio divina is very similar to the way you rest in God during centering prayer. If you are familiar with this contemplative resting, you may find yourself drawn into it right away as you gently and wordlessly absorb the passage.

Response Formats for Lectio Divina in Groups

In lectio divina, after listening to the passage read several times, sometimes you remain in silence, other times you are invited to respond from the heart. What does it mean to speak from the heart? You are listening to the passage with the ear of the heart and you can listen in the same way to your inner self. Listen for an inner voice from deep within. You may be surprised by what arises because it may not come to you in quite the same way as your ordinary thoughts.

If you are invited to speak, you share from this inner experience, usually using "I" statements. You might say "Today, for me, the passage brings up *this*," or "God seems to be saying *this* to me today through this passage." You allow your reflection to have personal resonance without making an argument for a particular "objective" interpretation. You do not comment on what others have shared or try to initiate a discussion. It is always all right to remain in silence if you choose.

This contemplative way of speaking may be unfamiliar to newcomers, who may at first want to respond in wordy, abstract, intellectual, impersonal ways that are more like what is expected in everyday speech. Because this kind of everyday discourse is natural and familiar, these kinds of responses may lead the whole group into a discussion that is not appropriate in the context of lectio divina. In order to protect the contemplative space it can be helpful to tailor the response format to the size and experience level of the group. However, even very experienced groups may prefer one of the less talkative formats.

Here are four different options for responding to a lectio divina passage:

Silent Lectio Divina—After the passage is read three or four times, there is no verbal response to the reading at all. This method works well for very large groups in which there is no time for responses or for groups who have difficulty avoiding intellectual responses.

Simple Lectio Divina, Word or Phrase Only—After the passage is read three or four times, the members of the group are invited to repeat a word or phrase from the passage that resonated for them. This method works well for large groups when there is not much time for everyone to speak, for groups who are having difficulty refraining from more intellectual discussion, or for groups who have many visitors who have not practiced lectio divina before. It can be surprisingly powerful to hear the words in the passage that resonated for others. This format offers an opportunity to respond and hear each other's voices while remaining very quiet.

A Few Sentences—After the passage is read three or four times, the members of the group are invited to share a few sentences of reflection. This method works well for small groups who understand that lectio divina is not about intellectual discussion and that no one should dominate the group with excessive talking. If you are experiencing problems with this method in a group, you might want to create and review some specific guidelines for the group, as described in the chapter "Guidelines for Sharing in Contemplative Groups."

Traditional Lectio Divina, based on the four movements—The facilitator reads the passage four times. Before each reading the facilitator might say a sentence or two to guide the group and remind them of what movement or section they're in:

1. **Listen**—Notice if any phrase, sentence, or word stands out and gently begin to repeat it silently to yourself, allowing it to touch you deeply.
2. **Reflect**—What might God be asking of you through the passage? You are invited to share a few words of reflection.
3. **Respond**—You are invited to offer a few words of prayer that are arising within you.
4. **Rest**—Just rest in God's presence, beyond thoughts or reflections.

Like the "few sentences" method, this method risks becoming too conversational, but can help participants understand and enter more deeply into the movements of lectio divina.

Discussion Afterwards

While it's best to avoid intellectual types of discussions *during* lectio divina, it can sometimes be helpful when doing lectio divina in a group to have a discussion time *after* the lectio divina when members of the group are free to raise more intellectual questions or talk about problems or questions they may have had about the passage that they were not comfortable raising during the lectio divina time. Such a discussion can help members to better understand the difference between intellectual discussion and the more reflective, contemplative nature of lectio divina.

Practicing Lectio Divina Alone

Lectio divina can also be practiced very fruitfully by an individual. You may find that practicing centering prayer or sitting in silence for a few minutes before looking at the passage will prepare you to listen with the ear of the heart. Read the passage at least twice, and often four times or more, with periods of silence in between. You might find that reading the passage aloud enables you to hear the passage more clearly. Each time you read the passage you may enter into it more deeply, allowing it to touch you and act upon you in a mysterious way. You may find it helpful to have a piece of paper handy to jot down reflections, prayers, and drawings while reading the passage. When practicing alone, you may find yourself led intuitively to practice lectio divina in a very particular and personal way that helps you to integrate the practice into the rest of your prayer life.

Choosing a Passage

To find scripture passages for use in lectio divina, you could begin with some of the passages in the "Readings" section of this book, or consult one of the books on lectio divina listed in "Resources," which contain passages or reference numbers for passages. Once you experience the types and lengths of scripture passages that work well, you may develop your own sense of what kind of passages will suit you and your group. Work your way slowly a few verses at a time through the Sermon on the Mount or another part of the Gospels; flip through and find a favorite passage with which you would like to spend more time; or consult a lectionary to find passages that are being read that week in church.

Lectio divina is not the same as spiritual reading, but has a more specialized meaning, referring to a particular way of reading a Bible passage. That being said, non-scriptural passages can be read in the lectio divina format, and this approach may often be appropriate for inclusive groups that are open to the wisdom of different traditions and voices. All three of the leaders of our group tend to be attracted to non-scriptural passages that are rooted in Christian tradition, for example passages from spiritual classics like Teresa of Avila or Symeon the New Theologian, or more modern writers like Thomas Keating or Thomas Merton. We are also very comfortable in our group with writings from other religious traditions, particularly Buddhism and Taoism, and with poetry. A group that is exploring its comfort level with non-scriptural passages might try alternating between scriptural and non-scriptural passages at its meetings. An advantage to rotating leadership in our group is that the three leaders have different taste in readings and we get to enjoy the freshness and surprise of each other's choices. Examples of some of our favorite passages are included in the "Readings" section.

In our group we tend to choose readings of about forty to two hundred words. Passages much longer than that can tire the reader and the practice begins to feel too wordy. We often read very short passages three or four times, longer passages only two or three times, at the discretion of the reader. However, it's helpful to announce at the beginning how many times you are planning to read so that others know what to expect. Some groups prefer very short readings, such as sayings of Jesus that are only ten or twenty words long, for example, "Judge not, that you not be judged," or "This is my commandment, that you love one another as I have loved you."

As you choose a passage for lectio divina from less traditional sources, you might ask yourself, "Does this passage help me remember what is important? Does it help me remember the presence of God, even if it doesn't use God language?"

It is possible to listen with the ear of the heart while not necessarily agreeing with the content of the passage. You may hear God speak to you even, or maybe especially, in readings that are challenging for you. No one has ever openly objected to one of the readings we've selected, but silence does not constitute agreement. In my recollection the loudest dissent we've heard after the group has been to biblical passages. No choice is safe, and perhaps that is not even a good goal. When God speaks to you through a passage, it is not always to affirm what is being read. You might receive an invitation to speak truth or stand up against injustice.

A Concise Guide to Visio Divina

VISIO DIVINA IS A FORM of divine seeing in which we prayerfully invite God to speak to our hearts as we look at an image. While lectio divina is a traditional way of reading a text with the ear of the heart, in visio divina, lectio's visual cousin, we look at an image with the eye of the heart. As we gaze, present to an image without any particular agenda, we allow it to speak to us in words or wordlessly with a divine voice.

As Gail Fitzpatrick-Hopler puts it:

> Visio Divina facilitates a relationship with an image or subject, patiently being with it, receptive in mind and heart, perhaps even in dialogue with it. In stillness, we allow the image to reach beyond the intellect and into the unconscious level of our being, a place that can't be accessed directly. In wonder, we are invited to look at every aspect of an image and ponder it as an encounter with God. It is a way of seeing an aspect of ourselves in God at the non-verbal, heart level. The canvas then becomes alive with personal meaning meant just for us. This is the same movement of the Spirit we can experience with Lectio Divina and Scripture.[x]

I often explore with people where they most feel the presence of the sacred in their lives, and many people mention nature and art as the places where they feel the greatest sense of meaning and aliveness. Yet while people feel drawn to the mysterious energy they experience in their favorite artworks, it often doesn't occur to them to see the cultivation of a relationship with this energy as a spiritual practice. Art can be a helpful entry point for those who are attracted to spiritual practice but not immediately comfortable with religious language. At workshops on visio divina there is often an atmosphere of excitement as people feel they are being given permission to take seriously the powerful feelings that art evokes in them. Throughout history, paintings and sculptures have been created for use in worship, to enhance sacred spaces and as portals to the divine, yet modern people often separate artworks from their sacred purpose by placing them in secular museums. After practicing visio divina for the first time and reconnecting with the sacred energy found in art, people have told me they'll never think about museums the same way again.

Practicing one or two periods of centering prayer before visio divina helps prepare participants to receive the image in a contemplative way. Groups who are accustomed to practicing centering prayer followed by lectio divina may find it refreshing to substitute visio divina for the lectio and may move easily into this practice since it bears so many similarities to lectio.

Choosing an Image

Choose a favorite piece of art, an icon, or a photograph. It doesn't need to be religious. Don't worry if you're not sure why you're selecting it. Does it vibrate with energy for you? Does it have a sense of mystery? Does there seem to be a story hidden within it? Does it evoke memories, emotions, a mood, or a feeling in your body?

Nowadays there are plenty of rich sources of imagery online, many in the public domain and freely available for use. If you will be printing or projecting an image for large-scale use, make sure you find a high-resolution version.

Instructions for Visio Divina

Visio divina is a form of divine seeing in which we prayerfully invite God to speak to our hearts as we look at an image. As you gaze at an image, you will be offered some questions for silent reflection, some of which may speak to you, while others you may choose to ignore. At the end of the visio divina, you will be invited to share a word or phrase to express your experience of the image.

As you gaze at the image, notice your breath and your body.

Simply be present to the image and allow it to speak to your heart, without any particular agenda. It might speak to you in words or wordlessly.

How do you feel looking at the image?

If you had to describe the image in a sentence or two silently to yourself, what would you say?

If you were in the image, where would you place yourself?

Do you get a glimpse of the sacred from this image?

Is God speaking to you in this image?

Does a name for God arise for you from this image?

In silence, sit with what you have received.

If you choose, share aloud a word or phrase to express your experience of the image.

When practicing visio divina in a group, it's helpful for the facilitator to leave a long pause between each question, using an intuitive sense of the appropriate length for the pause. Since this is a new experience for many, some people have told me that it's helpful when the silences aren't *too* long because they may start to feel lost. It's natural with this new way of praying to experience resistance or a sense of confusion: "I don't know how to do this!" Just trust the process as you would any other contemplative practice, knowing that by entering wholeheartedly into the experience you are saying *yes* to God's transformational presence.

As a facilitator I sometimes feel afraid that newcomers won't easily be able to enter into the practice. Yet again and again people are gently drawn in and I hear the power of their experience in the words they share. In the role of facilitator I often don't expect to experience much myself while I am busy reading the instructions to others, but the energy of this practice sneaks up and pulls me in. Once a contemplative atmosphere has been established it only takes a few moments for my gaze to enter the image and encounter the transcendent within.

Some groups, particularly small ones and ones that meet regularly, may choose to make the sharing portion of the experience longer and more open-ended. For such situations, you might find it helpful to review the section on response formats in the chapter "A Concise Guide to Lectio Divina" and guidelines for sharing in the chapter "Guidelines for Sharing in Contemplative Groups."

Displaying an Image

In contrast with the practice of lectio divina, which simply requires reading a text aloud, the practice of visio divina may pose more logistical challenges. How will the image be displayed? Here are several options, ranging from the simple to the more high-tech:

- **Use a large icon or poster**—Do you have a large image readily available that can be displayed to the group? Examples might include a framed picture, a poster on the wall, or a large icon on a stand. Could you print out an image from a computer that is large enough for the group to see, or print out multiple images that could be shared?
- **Display the image on a television or computer screen**—Many groups these days take place in a room where there is a television monitor. For these situations I often use an image found online, store it on my phone in presentation software, and use an HDMI adapter to connect the phone to the HDMI

cable on the television. The image could also be shown on the screen of a computer. If you are going to use one of these methods, set the preferences on your phone or computer so that it will show the image indefinitely without going to sleep while you are in the middle of presenting.

- **Postcard method**—I have a large selection of art postcards that I've collected from museums, art galleries, and historic places that people can sort through to make a selection. This method works well for a workshop when people will have some time in advance to flip through a pile of images to find one that has particular energy for them. If there is room, the postcards can be spread out on a table to make them easier to see as participants make their selections. With this method each person will be experiencing a different image, and choosing the image becomes part of the process. When less time is available, each person could be handed a card at random. I usually warn participants that they won't be able to keep the postcards at the end because otherwise people may become attached to items from my collection. Some participants may wish to photograph the images at the end to reflect on later.
- **Have an image specially printed**—For a special event, it is sometimes possible to have a postcard or smaller sized card specially printed. Online printers can make high quality color printing surprisingly affordable, at twenty-five or fifty cents per card. A short text such as the following might be printed on the back of the card so that it can be used at home.

A Contemplative Experience

Visio divina is a form of divine seeing, in which we prayerfully invite God to speak to our hearts as we look at an image.

Gaze at the image on this card, or another image you see, noticing your breath and your body. Simply be present to the image and allow it to speak to your heart, in words or wordlessly.

Ask yourself: Is God speaking to me through this image?

Offer a prayer, blessing, or reflection or simply rest wordlessly in what the image and your experience offer you.

Just be.

- **Show the image to an online group**—The chapter "Contemplative Prayer in a Digital Context" explores how to meet in a contemplative group using a video format. Visio divina is very easy to experience in this format because you can simply use the screen sharing function of the video software to project an image onto the screens of everyone in the meeting.
- **Practice in a gallery or museum setting**—If you have access to art hanging on walls in a gallery or museum setting you can invite a group to position themselves in front of a large artwork or row of artworks while you read them the visio divina instructions.

A Concise Guide to Walking Meditation

WALKING MEDITATION IS OFTEN USED as a way of stretching and refreshing the body, providing a break between periods of sitting in centering prayer, but it is an important practice in and of itself. As a dynamic practice it can help us to learn to bring our prayer into action and create a transition from our sitting practice to our everyday life.

Instructions for Walking Meditation

Place your hands in a comfortable position, perhaps hanging at your sides or lightly clasped at your waist. Begin to walk at a slower pace than usual, paying attention to your body and particularly your feet. Notice the sensation of lifting each foot and placing it back on the floor. Feel each step fully. If your mind begins to wander, bring it gently back to the sensations in your body, the feeling of moving through space, the feeling of the soles of your feet touching and leaving the floor.

In order to maintain awareness of your body, it can be helpful to maintain a stately posture, like a king or queen, not stiff but alert and graceful.

The great master of walking meditation, the Vietnamese monk and peace activist Thich Nhat Hanh, tells us that "we can arrive in the present moment with every step" and expresses the power of walking meditation in this passage from his book *How to Walk:*

> When I go to the airport, I like to arrive early so that I can do walking meditation before the flight. About thirty years ago I was walking in the Honolulu airport. Someone came up to me and asked, "Who are you; what is your spiritual tradition?" I said, "Why do you ask?" And he said, "Because I see that the way that you walk is so different than the way others walk. It's so peaceful and relaxed." He had approached me simply because of the way I walked. I hadn't given a speech or a conference. With every step you make, you can create peace within yourself and give joy to other people.[xi]

Walking meditation is often carried out in a circle around the outside of the chairs or cushions where the meditators have been sitting and can also be carried out outdoors. If you do not have room for walking meditation, you can invite the group to stand up and do a short, mindful stretch in between sitting sessions. You can also make clear in your instructions that no one is required to do walking meditation, especially since people with physical limitations are sometimes not able to do so.

At our church group in between two twenty-minute periods of centering prayer we process down a side aisle and up the center aisle towards the cross. I always enjoy the stately feeling of processing silently in the beautiful church space.

A Concise Guide to Chanting and the Psalms

I will sing to God as long as I live;
I will praise my God while I have my being.

—Psalm 104[xii]

We begin our group by chanting a psalm. The rhythm and breathing of the chanting bring us into our bodies and help us to settle down after the bustle of traveling to the group at the end of a work day. The ritual of chanting the Psalms connects us with centuries of monastic tradition. The chanting is like an entrance we walk through from the ordinary world into the prayer space.

Why the Psalms?

The Book of Psalms is a collection of one hundred and fifty ancient prayers considered scripture in both the Jewish and Christian traditions. Jesus, as a faithful Jewish man, prayed using the Psalms, and some of his most famous words, for example "My God, my God, why have you forsaken me?" and "Into your hands I commend my spirit," are quotations from the Psalms.

The Psalms express the full range of human emotion, including joy, despair, rage, vengefulness, fear, loneliness, gratitude, alienation, peacefulness, intimacy, weariness. They challenge us to pray honestly, exposing all of our thoughts and emotions to the gaze of God. They describe vengefulness and anger not because God encourages these things but because these emotions may be a part of our experience that we need to bring to God in prayer. In our more comfortable moments the desperate feelings that some of the Psalms describe may seem remote, but when injustice, misfortune, mental and physical illness, addiction, or even just the everyday pain of being a human being arouse these emotions, the Psalms are there to help us acknowledge them.

Many people dislike the Psalms and are uncomfortable with the way God is depicted within them. Yet at the same time they may be drawn to their poetry. The Psalms provide a road by which people may reapproach the religion of their youth. If you have rejected Christianity as too judgmental and intolerant, some of the images of God you see in the Psalms may reinforce this impression. Yet there may be something about Christianity that continues to draw you, embodied in the beauty, awe, and mercy expressed by the Psalms. The Psalms are a rich terrain where these attractions and discomforts can be explored. By eliciting conflicting and paradoxical feelings that can continue to exist in tension as part of the complex landscape of your life of prayer and belief, the Psalms provide a kind of laboratory of the soul. You don't have to solve the problem of the conflicting things that the Psalms evoke in you as you hold them in your prayer.

I used to hate the Psalms for their focus on enemies and their calls for vengeance to a God who seemed harsh and angry. Yet their poetry and grandeur kept drawing me back. In my work and in my own prayer life I see how much help most of us need in learning to pray to God with complete honesty. The Psalms invite me to express the fullness of my raw and messy feelings to God in my prayer. When I do, it changes me.

There are many different translations of the Psalms available which address potential discomforts with the language of the Psalms in a variety of ways. The very free adaptations by Stephen Mitchell, the well-known translator and poet, capture their beauty and power while omitting the most problematic of the Psalms. Nan Merrill's version substitutes language that emphasizes the loving nature of God. The sisters of the Order of St. Helena have created a version of the Psalms featuring fully inclusive language while remaining close to the traditional language of *The Book of Common Prayer*. Details of these adaptations are listed in "Resources."

Exploration of these different adaptations may embolden you to create your own versions of the Psalms that express your prayer to the God of your understanding. When I have encouraged people to edit the Psalms to make them more usable in prayer, they have sometimes discovered that if they try to throw the problematic parts out, later on they find they need them again, perhaps without even understanding why. The Psalms are truthful about the inner life in ways we may not always be ready for. As we become ever more honest about ourselves and our inner darkness we may find the Psalms more and more useful in our prayer.

Chanting the Psalms

The word "psalm" means song. The Psalms are intended for singing and have been sung for centuries in monasteries. Chanting is a kind of speech that uses musical tones while following the rhythms of ordinary speech. Anyone can chant a psalm. The simplest way is to chant in a monotone, a simple practice that does not require training, study, or a particularly good voice. It can be moving to hear the vulnerability of the human voice, revealing the fragility and finitude of the body. Through the poetry of the Psalms, the human voice expresses the reality of human existence in a vital, palpable way.

Like any spiritual practice, chanting requires a certain quality of attention. When you are fully present in your body giving your full attention to your task, your chanting may have an arresting quality in spite of or perhaps even because of the limitations of your voice.

Instructions for Monotone Chanting

Come fully into your body, taking a few deep breaths and noticing the sensation of your breath filling your lungs and torso. Take a few moments to still your mind so that you will be ready to give your full attention to your chanting. Choose a single note that is comfortable for you and chant the psalm in a monotone, using that single note. Emphasize words and phrases just as you would if you were reading aloud to a group, trying to make your phrasing lively and expressive. Even though you are chanting in a monotone there is no need to be monotonous.

When one person is chanting with confidence, it is generally easy for the rest of a group to follow along, even if they have never chanted before. In our group we use an antiphon, a short sentence excerpted from a psalm that is repeated as a refrain. We offer a choice of two antiphons, derived from the Psalms: "In the shadow of your wings I rejoice, alleluia," or "God whispers to the heart, 'Be still; I am with you.'" The Psalms with antiphons may be found in the "Program for a Regular Meeting" and the melodies we use to chant these two antiphons may be heard on my website (see "Resources") but these too may be chanted in a monotone. The leader chooses an antiphon, chants it once, then repeats it as the group joins in. The leader will then chant a few verses of the psalm, pause, and repeat the antiphon with the group following along. The regular participants become comfortable chanting the familiar antiphons while the leaders are free to vary the verses from the Psalms and the melodies from week to week if they choose. The most important thing is not so much the melody or monotone that is chosen but that the leader be clear about what is about to be chanted. If the antiphons are to be chanted using the same melodies each time, it can be helpful for the leader to make a recording on a cell phone of whatever melody is decided on in order to maintain consistency.

For a detailed exploration of how to chant the Psalms, I recommend Cynthia Bourgeault's book *Chanting the Psalms*, which describes many styles of chanting and comes with an instructional CD. The book includes a number of very simple chanting styles as well as more complex ones, demonstrated clearly on the CD. In our group we often use a version of what Bourgeault calls Modified Anglican Tone to chant the verses of our psalm.

Suggestions for Contemplative Home Practice

THE MOST IMPORTANT ASPECT of setting up a home practice is finding the motivation to practice every day. If you can't remember why your practice is important to you, then something else will always seem more pressing. You will always need a little bit more time for your work or your family or your own self-care. If you have the motivation, then you find the time and place. If your motivation falters, try going back to the essential practice of connecting with who God is for you right now, described in the chapter "Who Is God for You?" When you remain grounded in your own sense of the sacred, then you will be drawn to spend time in that presence, knowing that the sacred can nourish and support you and that the time devoted to your practice will ultimately be worthwhile.

Find a place in your home or office where you can be comfortable and quiet, if possible with a comfortable chair or cushion and door that can be closed. Make it clear to others that you need to be undisturbed during your prayer time. Think about what you need to create a sacred space welcoming to your prayer. Possibilities: candles, icons, incense, sacred objects, sacred books, quotations on the wall, art reproductions, art postcards, a bell to ring at the beginning and end of each session. Create a place that you associate with prayer and where you like to pray so that the prayer time is something you look forward to.

Have a timer available. Using a timer enables you to focus entirely on your prayer during the period allotted. You can use a simple egg timer or buy a dedicated timer. There are many apps available for smartphones and computers that can be used to time and track your meditation sessions.

Think carefully about what time of day will work best for your practice. It's easier to create a regular practice if you are able to pray at the same time each day. Many people find that if they get up a little early this provides them with a time when they are peaceful and undisturbed. The earlier in the day you pray the less likely that your prayer session will be swept away by the events of the day. I find the time I spend in centering prayer is so refreshing that it allows me to sleep a little less, if necessary. Other possibilities: when you first arrive at your office, when the kids have left for school, during lunch break, upon arriving home from work, last thing at night.

Set realistic goals. If you know from experience that you are completely unable to meditate for more than five minutes at a time, or that your schedule is so crazy during the week that you can only pray on the weekends, keep that in mind. It's good to challenge yourself and work on creating new habits, but don't set yourself up for certain failure. If you're unsure how much you will be able to do, you could set up a required practice that seems doable, plus an "extra credit" assignment that you could do if you have enough time. Or start with a doable goal, like five minutes of centering prayer a day, and then work up.

Five minutes is better than no minutes. The only bad prayer session is a skipped prayer session. If you find that you are unable to stick to your goals, don't give up entirely. Centering prayer can help us to acknowledge how much we need God. When we see how unable we are to let go of our thoughts, we recognize our limitations and our dependency on God. A few minutes in prayer can help us to stay connected to God, and God can use our limitations to draw us closer.

Twenty minutes twice a day is a good goal to aim for. A twenty minute period leaves enough time for a busy mind to settle down. Many people find that the last few minutes are the most peaceful and therefore they decide to move to two thirty minutes periods a day to enjoy extra stillness at the end of the sessions. The second period of prayer can be done in the middle or at the end of the day. I find that doing it after lunch refreshes me and makes me more clearheaded, energized, and centered for the afternoon ahead.

Meditation is hard work. Many people think that they are somehow worse at centering prayer than other people, but the truth is that most people find it difficult. Like anything else, it gets easier with practice, but even those who have been practicing for many years sometimes have difficult sessions. Everything you put into it you will get back. When it's hardest, that might be when you get the most out of it. Thomas Keating calls centering prayer the divine therapy because of the way it loosens the repressed emotional wounds of a lifetime. Sometimes when our prayer seems most turbulent, profound healing is taking place.

Many people find it much easier to maintain a home practice if they are practicing in a group once a week or at least every once in a while. The prayer of the other members of the group provides important support and the community offers an opportunity to ask questions and share concerns about the practice. Another option is to find a prayer partner. This might be someone who has a similar centering prayer schedule or someone who is interested in talking about the practice. Check in with each other on a regular basis and share concerns. Practice together when possible. If you can't find anyone in your area with whom to practice, see the chapter "Contemplative Prayer in a Digital Context" for ideas on how to practice with others in remote areas.

Prayer and meditation often send us into uncharted, disorienting territory. It's easy to feel like you're doing the centering prayer wrong because it's so unlike your other activities and because it's difficult to develop a new relationship with your thoughts. Don't be discouraged. Every day is a new day and a new opportunity to be close to God. God values your intentions and your desire to pray.

The Need for Community

In addition to some kind of practice, everyone needs some form of community in order to grow in contemplative maturity. Community doesn't need to mean a large, institutional community. Some people are able to develop very rich spiritual lives by meeting regularly with just a few people. Jesus promised that when two or three are gathered together in his name, he is there. A community can consist of a few trusted spiritual friends. However, it's important to be meeting and speaking regularly with others who share at least some of your beliefs and practices. Sometimes you don't even know what you feel and believe until you have an opportunity to speak aloud. As you struggle to figure out how to live from your beliefs and practices, you need feedback from others to help you stay on track and challenge you in constructive ways. It's easy to become misguided or to imagine that you are developing a great deal spiritually when not much is really happening. Talking about your beliefs and practices with others helps you to hear yourself clearly, work out your thoughts more thoroughly, and feel supported at difficult times.

Do you have the companionship that you need to support you and keep you on your spiritual path? Who will challenge you and be honest with you as well as encourage and affirm you? Who will see who you are and who you are in the process of becoming? Who knows your bad habits but also your potential? Who nourishes you with their presence? Who gives you an opportunity to speak your truth?

If you are not currently in a meaningful community, ask yourself if there is a church, temple, meditation center, or recovery group that has been calling to you. Perhaps you are already a member of a community but are uncomfortable there or standing on the sidelines and needing to take a step to become more deeply involved in a way that is right for you. Is there a person or persons in your life who might be able to help you to answer the questions you have about your spirituality and contemplative practice? If you already have a trusted friend of this kind, do you need to make an appointment to meet more regularly? If you live in an area where you're not meeting any like-minded people, can you find a digital community or class? Is there spiritual direction available to you, either individually or in groups?

Who can help you to listen to God's voice and how can you make such people a more regular part of your life? How can you move from the occasional, unexpected encounter with the holy into a community where you regularly feel connected with God and with those around you?

Guidelines for Sharing in a Contemplative Group

Talking about prayer and the inner life is a new experience for many people. In order to bring the same kind of attention to discourse that we bring to contemplative prayer we may need to learn a new way of speaking and listening. Spiritual sharing can be intense and even a bit frightening when we reveal things about our inner selves that leave us feeling tender and exposed. Everyday conversation has a kind of gravitational pull that tends to draw us back out of the contemplative space when we try to use the familiar habits of casual conversation to temper this more heartfelt way of talking and relieve the anxiety it may provoke. Clear guidelines for spiritual discourse can help us to create a safe environment and honor the nature of what is being said as we talk about the life of the spirit.

There are four different modes of discourse that might be used at one time or another in a contemplative group:

Regular conversation—Casual, everyday conversation tends to be unstructured and spontaneous, without limits on crosstalk and intellectuality. There are rarely any clearly defined guidelines. You can offer opinions and interrupt others as you choose. The group might use casual conversational style as the participants enter and leave, before and after the more formal meeting of the group. Alternatively, the group might decide that it prefers to convene and leave in silence.

Religious discussion—It's common to talk about spiritual and religious subjects in this same everyday manner. When you are having an intellectual conversation about theology you might allow for crosstalk and arguments, interrupt each other, and speak largely in terms of abstract ideas. A group might allow time for such a discussion *after* the formal conclusion of the prayer time when participants could discuss scholarly interpretations of the scriptural passage just used in lectio divina, debating the meaning of certain words, the sociological context, or the theological implications. Such a discussion is not appropriate *during* the lectio divina since it would lead away from speaking from the heart.

Lectio divina—The chapter on lectio divina has already described guidelines for use in that very particular form of interaction. In lectio divina you speak from the heart, letting go of more intellectual, studious, or effortful ways of thinking and entering a state in which you are quiet and receptive to God's voice. Listening for an inner voice from deep within yourself, you share from this inner experience, usually using "I" statements. Reflections during lectio divina tend to be short and simple depending on the size and experience of the group.

Spiritual sharing—Spiritual sharing is closely related to sharing in lectio divina, heartfelt and often quite structured, but may be lengthier and leave more room for spontaneity and digression. In its greater freedom there is more risk of being drawn back into everyday conversation. The leader must often be attentive and firm to help the group maintain the integrity of the sharing.

A few simple guidelines can protect this integrity, helping the group to speak in a more contemplative manner, from the heart, with an expectation that others will respond in kind.

Guidelines for Spiritual Sharing

- We listen attentively and without interruption when someone else is speaking.
- We share experiences from our own lives, not abstract ideas. We use "I" statements.

- We try to make sure that everyone has an opportunity to speak, but no one is required to. We do not lecture or dominate the group time with our own speaking.
- We do not give advice, criticize, or comment on what others share.
- We keep our sharing in the group absolutely confidential.

These simple guidelines encourage us to avoid crosstalk in which we speak casually back and forth. Without crosstalk we are more likely to listen carefully and openly instead of thinking about what we are going to say next. We are invited to speak from our own experience without assuming that we know all the answers and can solve other peoples' problems. These guidelines provide an opportunity for every participant to speak in a meaningful way if they so choose without having to aggressively push for a space for themselves in the conversation.

These guidelines may leave some of us feeling confused. How do we even have a conversation without giving advice or talking about abstract ideas? Doesn't being spiritual mean trying to fix or save other people? Our culture encourages us to speak in abstract language about an objective, universal reality that may not actually exist. In contrast, in spiritual sharing we are encouraged to speak from a subjective place. We might resist this as too personal, irrational, and overly revealing. However, if we speak out of our own experience we know we are speaking truth, whereas if we claim to speak about an objective, universal truth then we may seem to others to be trying to impose our own view of reality, insisting that we have some special knowledge that they don't have. When we speak from a more heartfelt place, safe in the knowledge that we won't be interrupted or criticized, we can feel ourselves gaining access to a deeper, wiser part of ourselves and allowing it to speak.

Formats for Spiritual Sharing

A group that is reading a passage from a contemplative book or viewing a video about centering prayer might be invited to reflect on questions like "How is God speaking to me through this reading?" or "How does this video relate to my spiritual practice?" Alternatively, if no reading or video is being used, the leader might give participants an opportunity to share more about their faith journeys by asking them to reflect on a question like, "Where do I feel the presence of God in my life right now?" or "How am I being called to become more fully myself?"

After asking the question, the leader might leave a few minutes of silence for reflection, then invite the group to share one at a time for a set period of time with brief silences in between. The leader can calculate how much time is available based on what time the group is scheduled to end, then divide by the number of people to determine how long each participant may share, including time for silence in between. This format ensures that each participant will have a chance to speak without being interrupted and without running out of time. The silences in between periods of sharing allow for further reflection and help make it clear that each participant is expected to speak out of their own experience rather than responding to what was previously said. The group may choose a pre-arranged order for sharing or allow the participants to choose when they will take their turns. The leader might issue a gentle warning a minute before each speaker's time is up to allow them to bring their sharing to a close.

This format may sound rather peculiar and formal but once it is experienced its similarities to contemplative practice become obvious. Indeed, it *is* a contemplative practice. Like any good ritual, its structure helps maintain a sense of the sacred. Candles, chanting, and prayers can also be used to set the tone and make it clear that you are inviting people into a special kind of discourse.

Format for Spiritual Sharing

- Question: Where do I feel the presence of God in my life right now? *or* How am I being called to become more fully myself?
- Several minutes of silence
- Sharing, with facilitator timing to ensure that each person will have time to share and offering a gentle warning a minute before each speaker's time is up
- One minute of silence
- Next sharing, until each person has an opportunity to speak, but no one is required to
- Closing silence or prayer

Of course the group might choose to use a far more casual format for sharing, but it can be useful to know that this structured method exists and is helpful in maintaining a safe and sacred atmosphere.

Guidelines could be discussed and agreed upon in an introductory meeting. In open groups in which participants come and go, changing often, it can be hard to set guidelines in place in an explicit way. If there is no introductory meeting attended by all participants then there may be no appropriate opportunity to discuss and agree upon a set of guidelines and not everyone in the group may be aware they exist. However, the leader could provide them and distribute them in printed form or post them online for easy reference, and if a problem arose the leader would be able to read them aloud or invite all participants to go back to them.

By gently but firmly enforcing the guidelines, the leader protects the contemplative space and helps participants be fully present to themselves and each other. If members of the group regularly dominate the conversation or digress inappropriately, the facilitator can use the guidelines to prevent the group from sliding into everyday discourse and patiently educate those who are not familiar with the guidelines or don't understand them. Without this safe structure many people will not feel able to share from a deep and heartfelt place. Why speak our truth if no one is really listening or if someone is going interrupt or to try to fix us? The guidelines provide a tool for bringing into the light the dynamics of what is happening in the group and maintaining an atmosphere in which participants feel safe and heard.

While gently helping the group to follow these guidelines, the leader can also be a participant in the group rather than standing apart from it. This participation increases the sense of trust, inclusion, and equality within the group. If the leader speaks too much like an "expert," it can erode the sense that the members of the group are all speaking from the heart and create a sense of hierarchy that makes others less eager to offer their own deepest reflections. As a leader you will be most effective when you can guide the group and share your own experience and possibly greater knowledge of the practices while also acknowledging that you are a companion on the same journey. This balance requires experience and humility.

In addition to setting the tone for contemplative discourse, guidelines can also be useful to clarify other aspects of a contemplative group's format. The guidelines can become a kind of mission statement that describes the character and goals of the group. Below is an example of guidelines that were tailored over time to spell out the parameters of the contemplative prayer group at Grace Church Brooklyn Heights. Even if you don't use guidelines like these in an explicit way and make them available to the group in written form, it can be very helpful for the leader to have a clear, written set of guidelines which can be referred to when people ask questions or if a problem arises. These particular guidelines are not recommended for all groups but represent an example of the kinds of choices a group might make as it defines its own character and goals.

Example of a Longer, Customized Set of Group Guidelines

Grace Church Brooklyn Heights Group Guidelines:

- The group meets from 7 PM to approximately 8 PM on Tuesdays.
- The group usually meets from the second week of September through the first week of June and breaks for the summer. It does not meet during the weeks of Thanksgiving, Christmas, or in the first week of January.
- The group is open to anyone who would like to attend. Members may come as frequently or as infrequently as they would like.
- The Hicks Street entrance is only open from 6:45 until 7:15, so please arrive during that time. After 7:15 the door will be locked and we will not be able to open it without disrupting the group. If you enter after 7 PM please do so quietly.
- During the lectio divina, we listen in a prayerful way and speak from our hearts. We avoid an intellectual discussion. If anyone has anything to say that feels like it might not fit into the lectio format, discussion after the group might be a good time to share this. We do not interrupt each other during the lectio and we do not judge or criticize each other. We speak out of our own experience. We resist the urge to give advice or fix things. We listen to each other with respect. If anyone would like to speak more than once, he or she may do so.
- No one is required to speak or to share anything if he or she is not comfortable doing so.
- It is not necessary to make eye contact during the group.
- We maintain confidentiality about what is shared in the group.
- Lindsay Boyer, Jim Connell, and David James are the primary facilitators of the group, rotating regularly.

Part II

A Concise Guide to Contemplative Leadership

What Does It Mean to Be a Contemplative Leader?

Perhaps you are not even consciously planning to lead a contemplative group and yet you are reading this chapter and wondering what it might be like to be a leader in a contemplative context. Perhaps there is something in you that is trying to come into being and you sense that leading a contemplative group will somehow take you further along your path. Yet you might feel reluctance, imagining that leadership of a contemplative group requires some special worthiness. Aren't spiritual leaders supposed to be blameless moral people with great wisdom to share? In spite of these feelings of unworthiness you might continue to feel a sense of call or purpose.

Leadership can be an act of great simplicity. There's humility in being willing to lead even when you don't feel worthy. You see what is needed and are ready to do it. Perhaps there is no one better than you available for this task. Perhaps you would simply like to attend a group, can't find one in your area, and so you need to start one in order to attend. Leadership doesn't need to be a putting forward of yourself for self-centered reasons. You take it on not when you finally overcome all your human limitations but when you acknowledge that you never will. When the people in the group reveal their profound insights and prayerfulness, you might feel embarrassed to have taken the role of leader, but you are not putting yourself above them. You are serving them.

As you consider the possibility of leadership, you could articulate your questions and concerns in prayer without trying to answer them right away, allowing them to ripen within you. You might discuss the matter with a trusted friend or guide or reach out to an experienced mentor who might be willing to advise you. If you continue to feel you require more qualification, you could participate in a training program. Contemplative Outreach offers training for group facilitators and for those who would like to teach introductions to centering prayer. Or you might just go ahead, with a growing sense that God has no one but you right now for this particular task, trusting that God and others will guide and support you and that if you are on the wrong track you will learn more through your prayerful practice.

If you do not feel you are at the center of the community where you feel called to lead, this does not have to be a problem. For some of us, leadership is the way we find ourselves drawn into belonging. I began the group at Grace Church Brooklyn Heights when I was not attending the church regularly, was grateful to be welcomed, and now find myself an important part of the church in this very particular way.

It can be a big commitment to lead a group every week and a big help to the main facilitator if other participants are willing to at least substitute from time to time if not co-lead. However, people are often strangely reluctant to help out, perhaps experiencing the same sense of unworthiness with which the leader may be struggling. Participants may sometimes be coaxed into helping when it becomes clear that their assistance will allow the group to meet more regularly. I have been fortunate to find willing substitutes in the first years of our group and in more recent years two co-leaders with whom I rotate leadership on a weekly basis. This has made the group much stronger in that it enables us to meet more regularly and because each leader brings different skills and tastes.

As you form and facilitate a group I encourage you to follow your own intuition. As you go forward making decisions about the format of the group you can't always please everyone. Sometimes when there are differing needs and desires within a group, a decision must simply and somewhat arbitrarily be made by the leader. In some cases it makes sense to mix it up a bit and try different things on different occasions and sometimes the leader can learn from going with a consensus that differs from her own view, but sometimes the leader may feel called to follow her own vision for the group.

What motivates you as the leader? What keeps you wanting to lead and create sacred space for others? You are there to serve, yet in many cases the group would not be there without your service, so what helps you to continue to have the energy to lead the group week after week? Sometimes the best decisions are not self-sacrificing but rather help to energize and support the leader without whom the group would not exist.

Contemplative groups need a leader who will protect the contemplative way of being and prevent the group from sliding into everyday discourse. Yet at the same time the group works best when the leader is also a participant in the group rather than standing completely apart from it. The leader must find her own way to balance authority, honesty, and vulnerability, and the skill this requires comes with time, experience, and mentorship.

Presence

As leaders, we offer the group our spiritual presence. What does this mean? There are different kinds of spiritual presence. The first is quite simply and literally our physical presence. This has greater value than might at first be apparent. Even when participants come infrequently, it can be important to them to know that week after week you are there. Even when they are not attending, they could be. Their world is changed by the knowledge that there is a place where they could bring their prayer, where you are praying when they are not there.

You can also offer your priestly presence. When I use this term, I'm not just referring to those of us who are priests. I'm not a priest, but I believe that my own priestly presence is an important part of my work as a spiritual director and as a contemplative group leader. Christians are taught to be humble and obedient, and this can sometimes make us hesitant to embody the powerful presence that may help others step into their own authority. The word *persona* comes from the theatrical masks that were worn in ancient drama. As a spiritual leader, you may sometimes need to wear a mask, not a mask that hides you in a dishonest way but a mask that allows you to reveal yourself in a powerful way, like a holy garment. By wearing a priestly persona you can inhabit your spiritual role with a confidence and authority that enables you to sanctify space that might otherwise seem ordinary and bless people in ways that encourage them to approach the world with hope and dignity, believing in God and in themselves.

There is also the presence of your prayer, almost as if it were a separate entity. Through your contemplative practice you can develop a kind of reservoir of attentiveness and prayerfulness and make this deeply nourishing resource available to yourself and others. Your practice increasingly allows God to act through you, without your understanding. You may feel you are not doing enough. Contemplative practice helps you to strip away this sense of needing to do and come closer to being pure presence. If you are with others in a prayerful way, your loving, nourishing presence may convey something of God's loving presence, in spite or even because of your human limitations and what you think you are not able to offer. Maybe you've encountered people who you've experienced as pure presence, right when you needed it most. As your leadership deepens, you may increasingly find that prayer and silence help to strip away what is not needed until nothing is left but presence.

Starting a Contemplative Prayer Group

A CONTEMPLATIVE PRAYER GROUP, no matter how small, can be extremely helpful to its participants. It can provide a supportive community, strengthen the resolve of the participants to continue in their practice and help them go deeper into their prayer. It can also be an important formative experience to put together and facilitate a group.

Just Begin!

To start a group, all you need is a regular time slot and a room where you can sit comfortably and quietly without being interrupted.

Where to Meet

A sacred space can be created by the prayer itself anywhere there is room to meet. Our group is usually held in a chapel area in our church sanctuary where we are able to arrange chairs around a circular altar. However, I've also attended wonderful groups where we have been crowded into tiny offices or made comfortable in spacious meeting rooms with sofas. There's no reason the group has to meet in a church. A group may happily meet in a home or an office after hours. Sometimes a convenient, easily accessible location is more important than ambience. A candle and dim lighting can help create the proper atmosphere but are not necessary. Churches may be very helpful in making space available at no cost, but I also know of groups that rent space from retreat centers and ask for a small suggested donation from members to make up the rental charge.

When I began our group at Grace Church Brooklyn Heights I hoped to make the group more welcoming to those who might not be entirely comfortable in church by meeting in a somewhat neutral meeting room. However, the meeting rooms were constantly booked and we ended up in the church sanctuary, which seemed to influence the flavor of our group. While some contemplative prayer groups take on a format that is more like a class, with instruction, videos, and discussion, ours became more and more liturgical, filled with psalms, chanting, and candles.

I grew up in the Episcopal Church with chanting, bells, and incense. As a spiritual director I discovered to my surprise that when someone who was uncomfortable with religion wanted to try Buddhist meditation, if I recommended both a meditation center with a more neutral atmosphere and a Soto Zen service, full of candles, incense, chanting, and gongs, the person would almost invariably prefer the smells and bells. Although today many people hold intellectual and sometimes well-founded objections to religious dogma, they may at the same time have a deep, unsatisfied need for religious ritual. I rediscovered this hunger for ritual in myself and the other members of our group as we were drawn towards chanting and candles. Others may also find that the backgrounds and natures of participants and the flavor of their meeting spaces cause their groups to evolve in unexpected directions.

Although at one time I had gone to services at Grace Church regularly, at the time I started a group there I rarely attended and barely knew the new rector, who nevertheless welcomed our group with open arms. If you are interested in starting a group in a church but don't have an official church affiliation you may find that a church near you would welcome a new contemplative prayer group or that an existing group would welcome your support. Don't be discouraged if the first church you approach is not interested. Pastors and other church leaders may be grateful to be offered a clearly outlined program by a responsible individual and generous with church space when they appreciate that a contemplative group will enrich the prayer life of their community.

Group Size

Don't worry if your group is very small; the small size of the group may make the people who do come feel more comfortable. Centering prayer is simple but challenging, and many people may try the group but not stay. The group will be very valuable for those who do come, even those who don't come regularly, and sometimes even for those who only come one time.

The Contemplative Outreach website provides a great way to publicize a contemplative group. You could also set up a small website or Facebook page to let participants know about programs and schedule changes. Sponsoring guest speakers or programs about contemplative prayer, such as quiet days or introductions to centering prayer, can be a good way to attract new participants.

A Welcoming Atmosphere

We welcome everyone to our group as long as they are willing and able to sit in silence with us. At the beginning of each session we read this welcoming statement:

> Welcome to the Grace Church contemplative prayer group. This is a place for all God's people. Whatever your beliefs or doubts you are always welcome here. If you are new to centering prayer, just follow the instructions as the evening unfolds. You are also welcome to use the silence in any other way that is right for you.

Our group is a place where anyone can sit in silence and not worry about their beliefs or whether or not they are a Christian. We don't ask each other a lot of questions and people don't need to reveal anything they are uncomfortable about. A woman once told me that she was tired of "men talking too much" and that our group was the one place in her life where she didn't have to worry about having to listen to too much talking. Our group has always been open to anyone who would like to sit in silence with us. We try to make a place where those who are dominated or marginalized in other parts of their lives may find a respite. Over the years our group has attracted many people who have been practicing Buddhist and other kinds of meditation and are curious to try centering prayer or perhaps just find our group conveniently located for sitting in silence and doing other forms of meditation. We welcome latecomers, early leavers, snorers, and those whose physical conditions require them to adopt unusual postures.

There are also groups who after an initial formation period choose to close their membership so that they can share with greater intimacy or study readings that might not be appropriate or interesting to newer members.

How Much Silence Should Your Group Offer?

Many contemplative prayer groups are more talkative than ours. Other groups sometimes read passages from books about centering prayer such as *Open Mind, Open Heart* and offer reflections on how the readings relate to the participants' practices and lives. Others show a video each week of Thomas Keating exploring an aspect of centering prayer, followed by reflections from the group. These more conversational formats allow participants to study the practice while getting to know more about each others' journeys.

Though we associate intimacy with talking and getting to know each other, there's also great intimacy to be found in silence. Silence offers an important tool for building community with each other as well as with God. In our more silent group we have found that small talk and extensive sharing are not necessary to know each other. Yet there is something confusing and hard to believe about this experience because it is so countercultural. Many visitors to our group can feel this intimacy when they are with us but perhaps forget it when they leave.

Books and videos can help take us deeper into contemplative practice but experience of the practice itself is most important.

Setting too much stock in what others have to say about the practices may sometimes interfere with our own profound understanding of what the practices have to offer us. In our group we believe that silence is often enough. We trust it and listen to its voice.

These issues of silence versus talking pervade every aspect of a contemplative group. How much do you try to make people comfortable and how much do you offer them silence, which may make them uncomfortable but has much to teach them? How much do you explain the practice in each session, particularly to newcomers? Do you offer one period of centering prayer or two? In the lectio divina, do you ask people to offer a word or phrase or invite lengthier reflections? At the end of the program, do you sit and talk or put on your coats and go? Do you engage in a lengthy discussion with the person who always wants to talk about theology and Bible history or do you smile, respond briefly, and politely change the subject? Do you give preference to the tastes of the regular participants in designing the program or try to make the group accessible to visitors?

There are no right answers to these questions. In our group we have chosen a program that feels right for us, in keeping with our understanding of contemplative practice. I emphasize its strengths because it is a program that I know and trust and also because it is unusual, countercultural, and perhaps requires an advocate more than does a more conversational approach. However, I want to encourage group facilitators to explore a personal sense of call about how to lead and to discern what path is right for their group. The chapter on "Guidelines for Sharing in a Contemplative Group" addresses these questions in more detail as it investigates ways of speaking from the heart during group reflection.

Planning and Leading a Contemplative Quiet Day

We can become deeply depleted and disconnected from the source of our being when we allow our culture and schedules to tempt us into ever greater levels of busyness. Many people long for greater periods of silence, reflection, and spiritual practice but have trouble making room in their packed schedules. A quiet day can be a refreshing time to step back and hear what our hearts have been trying to tell us through all the noise. What do we need? What do we want? We may have been rushing around so busily that we no longer know. Out of silence a still, small voice can arise and be heard.

There are many ways to offer a quiet day. I will use my own experience as an example, not because it is ideal, but in order to make this chapter as specific, practical, and vivid as possible. When I was learning from David Frenette how to lead a retreat, we would review in advance how each aspect of the retreat would unfold. No detail was too small for us to consider. This preparation enabled us to visualize and anticipate many eventualities so that we were ready to hold the space for the participants in a prayerful and hospitable way. I offer the details of this chapter in the same spirit. While you may end up making your quiet day quite different from what is described here, I hope these practical details will help you picture everything in advance.

Creating a Quiet Container

The most important part of the quiet day is the quiet. Resist the temptation to pack too many activities and talks into the schedule. Our culture bombards us with information and stimulation, and the quiet day is a time for a change of pace. Silence, spiritual practice and unstructured time can make up the core of the day. Leaving unstructured time for participants to do nothing creates a spacious feeling and allows for the possibility that participants' prayerfulness and playfulness will emerge in spontaneous and unexpected ways.

I usually allow at least an hour for a silent lunch during which people can eat, read, journal, nap, and reflect while enjoying the unusual experience of being with others without needing to talk to them. Often people tell me that this silent lunch is their favorite part of the day, reminding me that while the success of the quiet day can be enhanced by my careful planning, it is not dependent on my doing. Talks and activities can be kept short and simple.

Your role as facilitator is to hold the space for the participants by creating a welcoming environment in which they have permission to refresh themselves, turn off their cellphones, and listen within. The expression "holding the space" might at first might seem like a figure of speech but describes a quality that participants can feel when they enter an environment that provides a hospitable container for whatever might be taking place within them. As a quiet day facilitator, you offer simple activities, many of which may be optional, not to fill up the time with stimulation but to structure the day so there is room for God to speak. You provide tools and suggestions that encourage attentive listening and discernment. You let participants know what to expect but also leave room for what is arising within them. While providing a structuring format for the day, you are ready to let go of this format if necessary when you sense that something else fruitful might take place. You work to create a safe atmosphere where people can experience all their thoughts and emotions without feeling judged. Rather than placing the emphasis on your own teaching and offerings, you help participants to trust their own wisdom and ability to hear the Spirit speak to them out of the silence.

As the leader of a quiet day you play an essential role simply by inviting people to take time apart during which God can speak to their hearts. You might have feelings of inadequacy about your qualifications for this work, but you can trust that your hospitality will allow the Spirit to enter the space and guide you and the participants. As you plan and lead the day, stay in touch with your own longings and sense of calling. What do you hunger for? What can you offer from your heart? You could host a speaker, and that may sometimes be appropriate, but perhaps you don't need to. The more I offer quiet days, the more I find that I can let go of the need to plan a lot of content and activities and let a very simple day, filled with silence and prayer, stretch out with welcoming arms.

Centering Prayer as a Foundation of the Quiet Day

Many people come to a quiet day thirsting for deep inner quiet but don't know how to find it. I always use centering prayer as the foundation of a quiet day, not only because it is part of my own personal daily practice and a gift I want to offer to others, but because it is a tool that helps participants to access the deep inner quiet they are seeking. Participants who taste this silence on the quiet day are grateful to be given a method they can use at other times in their lives to be in relationship with God and bring the quiet home with them.

I usually offer a brief introduction to centering prayer towards the beginning of the day, perhaps half an hour long, before the first centering prayer period. If you're not comfortable offering a brief introduction, you could simply review the basic guidelines of centering prayer or show a short video. (See "Resources.") If you are going to use some kind of contemplative practice as part of the quiet day it's usually good to offer a brief review no matter who your audience is, to refresh the practice of the more long-time practitioners and to support those who are new to the practice. I find that even if I publicize an event as being for more experienced practitioners, at least one newcomer often shows up.

You could also invite someone from Contemplative Outreach to come do a day-long introduction to centering prayer, which is a service that organization is happy to provide, usually free of charge, if there is a presenter available in your area. This is a fantastic way to introduce a group to centering prayer and refresh the practice of more longtime practitioners. This makes for a different kind of day than the quiet day discussed here, with less silence and a heavier emphasis on presentation and absorbing the teaching on centering prayer. Contact your local Contemplative Outreach chapter leader for more information. (See "Resources.")

Planning the Day

Who will attend your quiet day? The publicity for your quiet day will depend on your intended audience. You might offer the day to members of a specific church or meditation center that will help you publicize it. A day offered to the contemplative community within a certain geographical area could be publicized through Contemplative Outreach or another contemplative organization. A private group might choose not to publicize. I lead quiet days at Grace Church Brooklyn Heights that are offered to the parish through its e-newsletter but also to the wider contemplative community through the Contemplative Outreach of New York City e-newsletter and Facebook page. I am also fortunate to have a friend at the local Brooklyn paper who will often help publicize the quiet days. Other groups might not choose to publicize so widely.

The length of the day might depend on your own stamina and how long participants can conveniently stay. I have found that a five-hour schedule from 10 AM to 3 PM suits my own energy level as long as I don't do too much talking and have the opportunity to refresh myself with plenty of contemplative prayer. Longer than that and I have found that participants often start to need to leave early, which can be disruptive and tells me that perhaps a five-hour period is just the right length. Saturday usually seems to be the most convenient day for many people.

The day before the quiet day, I usually order a simple lunch of sandwiches, fruit, and water from a local store. The lunch costs approximately $12 per person and I usually ask for a suggested donation of $20, which is easy for people to put in a basket without the need to make change, unless for some reason I need to ask for a larger donation to cover other kinds of costs. The $8 difference gives me a little bit of a cushion in case there are participants who are unable to pay for lunch or in case participants who have signed up don't show up and I am left with unpaid-for lunches. There is often a flurry of last minute sign-ups and cancellations that makes it hard to predict final numbers with accuracy. I usually order two extra lunches to cover last minute drop-ins. I used to order box lunches but I now order sandwich halves on a plate, which seems to work out better when the number of attendees does not match the number who signed up since some people want only half a sandwich.

Sample Description for a Newsletter

Day of Centering Prayer and Visio Divina
Grace Church Brooklyn Heights
254 Hicks Street
Brooklyn NY 11201
Saturday May 18th, 10 AM – 3 PM

This day of centering prayer will begin with a brief review of the practice. We will spend most of the rest of our time in centering prayer with a break for lunch in silence. We will also engage in experiences of visio divina, a form of divine seeing in which we prayerfully invite God to speak to our hearts as we look at an image.

Recommended for anyone who would like to spend a day in centering prayer practice. A $20 donation is requested to cover the cost of lunch and to help us sponsor future events, but if you are unable to pay for the lunch, please come anyway!

For more information or to RSVP, contact Lindsay at mail@lindsayboyer.com.

Sample Email to Those Who Have Signed Up to Attend

Dear ———,

Thanks for signing up for the quiet day on Saturday May 18th from 10 am to 3 PM. I'm looking forward to seeing you! Please plan to arrive before 10 am. We will meet in the North Room. As you come through the 254 Hicks Street entrance, go up the stairs and turn right to find it.

Please plan to leave your cell phone turned off and not make any calls during the retreat time so that you can give yourself the gift of leaving the outside world behind for a brief period. Lunch will be provided so that you will not need to leave the retreat space during the retreat and we will eat in silence. This will allow you to have some sabbath time. Please let me know if you will not be able to attend or if you do not want the lunch so that we can order the right number of lunches. We will ask for a suggested donation of $20 to cover the cost of lunch, but if you are unable to pay for the lunch, please come anyway!

You're welcome to bring cushions, blankets, or anything else that might allow you to sit comfortably yet alert during the centering prayer. You might also want to bring a journal for writing down reflections about your experience. There is some parking information below for those who might be driving.

I'm hoping that our time together will be nourishing, healing, and contemplative for you. Please don't hesitate to contact me with any questions or concerns.

Blessings,
Lindsay

Setting Up for the Quiet Day

I usually arrive for the day at least a half hour in advance and post signs I've printed to help participants find the room. I set up a basket for donations, with a sign saying "Suggested Donation $20"; a clipboard for those who would like to be added to our mailing list; handouts; and any brochures we might be distributing about contemplative practices or events. For myself I set up a singing bowl or chime for the meditation, my phone or a timer, my notes, any readings I might be using to introduce meditation periods or for lectio divina, and my phone charger in case my phone runs low from timing meditation or showing slides. If I am not traveling too far I also bring a small suitcase full of some of my favorite books on spiritual subjects for participants to peruse while they are waiting for the day to begin and during the silent lunch, particularly books on contemplative prayer, vocation, poetry, books of religious art, and anything particularly relevant to the day's theme. While the books are mine and participants can't take them home, they are often extremely appreciative of the opportunity to flip through these new resources, almost like they are meeting new spiritual friends, and look forward to ordering them later.

I also bring art supplies such as paper, crayons, colored pencils, and oil pastels. Sometimes I will lead a guided meditation and invite participants to draw what they visualized in the meditation, and the art supplies are available as another tool that people can use during the unstructured time to process their reflections and allow themselves to become dreamy and spontaneous. These art supplies are very appealing to some people, inviting them to unleash a certain part of themselves. Others may resist the presence of the art supplies yet discover something valuable in themselves if they are nudged to use them in a playful, non-judgmental way.

I make sure there are enough chairs set up for the number of participants expected, usually somewhere between twelve and thirty, plus a few extras. The space where I usually hold the quiet day has a selection of sofas, soft chairs, and hard chairs, plus a few cushions that may be helpful for people with physical challenges.

If I am going to be using slides, I hook my phone up to a television monitor and test it to make sure I can get it to work. If I am meeting at Grace Church Brooklyn Heights a sexton kindly helps me set up chairs, television, tables for lunch, and coffee. At other locations I will sometimes purchase coffee boxes from a nearby store and set those up.

Getting the Quiet Day Started

I begin the day with a brief prayer, either extemporaneous or one I have written in advance to incorporate the themes of the day. I then orient the participants by taking them through the day's schedule and making sure they have a handout that might include the schedule, the basic guidelines of centering prayer, information on other contemplative practices we might be exploring, discernment questions that they can reflect on if they choose, quotations on themes of the day for inspiration, instructions for mindful eating, and my name and contact information. They are told where the bathrooms are and I ask if they have any logistical questions.

Next I usually ask participants to go around the room and say their names and a sentence or two about why they are there. This helps me to know what they are looking for and their level of experience with contemplative prayer. It grounds us and helps us to build a sense of community to hear each others' names and voices. Participants' brief comments take the emphasis off the facilitator and are often very inspiring in the way they give a snapshot of spiritual longings.

Coming apart from our busy lives and entering the quiet can make some people feel anxious, and it can be helpful to address this anxiety directly at the beginning of the day. I remind people that the Judeo-Christian tradition not only invites us but *commands* us to take time for sabbath to rest and refresh ourselves. This quiet time makes space for us to enter more deeply into relationship with God and our own deepest being. Sometimes life gets on top of us and we lose touch with our sense of our inner wholeness. The quiet day allows us to turn our attention towards the wisest part of ourselves and spend some time with it, listening and attending to it, remembering who we are and who God is for us.

I ask participants, "Can you remember a moment when you experienced God, in a surprising way, in a vivid way, in a way that changed you? A moment when you were in touch with God and with the deepest, wisest part of yourself? Perhaps this was a moment in childhood or a more recent moment, in nature, in church, looking at an artwork, or dancing. A time when you had a feeling of ease or transcendence or oneness with something outside yourself. Feel this moment. Taste it. What does it feel like in your body? What are the sights and sounds that you associate with this feeling? Let's make some space today for the part of yourself that you are feeling and tasting. Spend some time with it and reflect on how to nurture and protect it. And if you didn't experience much just now, I invite you to simply trust that God is at work in the way you have made the effort to come here today and open yourself to this new experience."

Themes for the Day

Are there specific themes your group would like to explore? What would most help your participants to quiet down so that they can hear a still, small voice? What are you longing to offer others that has touched you?

While I always include centering prayer in my quiet days, I usually add another element that gives the day a particular focus. This does not necessarily mean restructuring the schedule very much. It's more a matter of giving a brief talk at the beginning of the day on the theme, adapting the discernment questions and quotations on the handout and the lectio divina readings to reflect the theme, and perhaps adding additional contemplative practices to the schedule in a way that flows out of the centering prayer.

Some themes I have used include: lectio divina, visio divina, discernment, praying with the Psalms, spiritual practices for difficult times; healing; finding support for your spiritual journey; a contemplative day incorporating a contemplative Eucharist;

listening; spirituality and creativity; spiritual direction. You could also create a "Day of Centering Prayer" that has no additional theme, focusing on the practice in a simple way.

Instructions for Silent Lunch

Right before we break for lunch I offer guidelines for being in the silence. Unstructured time can make some people feel uneasy, including the facilitator, who may feel the need to be doing more. I ask people to remain as silent as they can but to be ready to make exceptions when they have a practical need to ask or answer a question. I urge them not to use their cellphones if at all possible. Unless the quiet day is taking place in a environment where participants can walk outside in nature, it's best if they can resist leaving the premises, which can be challenging on a pretty day, but particularly in urban environments or crowded places can cause people to be drawn into talking and ordinary life. Books and discernment questions are provided and journals can be used for reflection. But the greatest gift people can give themselves in the unstructured time is the space to just be, with no agenda. I invite them to let themselves enter a dreamy state in which unexpected thoughts, memories, and fantasies can float up and tell them what their hearts are longing for.

Some participants might appreciate being given instructions for eating in a mindful manner so that the eating itself becomes a meditative practice. However, it should be noted that there is some tension between the dreamy state mentioned above and the more bright and alert state of mindfulness. Do you want to encourage participants to rest and dream, allowing thoughts to float freely across their minds, or challenge them to pay attention? You might offer participants a choice. If these instructions are offered in the handout, they can always be used on another occasion.

Instructions for Mindful Eating

Bring yourself fully into your body, noticing your breath going in and out, gently letting go of thoughts that do not have to do with eating and being present to your food. If you are planning to give yourself fully to mindful eating, it is best to eat without reading, talking, or engaging in any other task as you eat.

Notice the colors, shapes, and textures of the food before you.

Slowly begin to eat, pausing to notice the sensations of the food and the feelings in your body as you eat and interact with your food.

Notice any thoughts that are coming up and gently let go of them if they do not have to do with the experience of eating.

Listen to your body. How do you feel as you eat? Does your body tell you when it has had enough?

Finally, offer a prayer for all those humans and creatures who helped bring your food to the table.

Reflections on the Day

Towards the end of the day it's important to leave time for participants to reflect on their experience. You can leave this very unstructured, simply asking anyone who chooses to share whatever came up for them during the day. Alternatively, you can ask participants to go around the room and each share something about what the day was like for them, which gives a gentle nudge to those who might choose to remain quiet. Some people may find it difficult to speak after a day of silence; they have not yet fully emerged from the quiet zone. Another question you can ask is, "What was most helpful about this day and what could have been better?" This question opens a door to share anything but can be taken in a less personal way by those who do not feel like sharing anything very personal and can yield a trove of information for you as you go forward planning more quiet days. I often close either with a prayer or by asking each participant to think of one word that encapsulates their experience of the day. We go around the circle saying our words, which creates a prayer-like ritual.

Sample Schedules

Here are sample schedules for two typical quiet days. The first is focused primarily on centering prayer and could be oriented towards somewhat more experienced practitioners. The second is designed to introduce participants to two contemplative practices, centering prayer and visio divina, and to accommodate both beginners and more experienced practitioners.

Schedule A	**Day of Centering Prayer**
10:00–11:00	Introduction to the day Brief centering prayer refresher Questions and comments
11:00–12:00	Two twenty-five-to-thirty-minute periods of centering prayer, with either walking meditation or a brief stretch in between
12:00–1:00	Lunch in silence Reflection, discernment, reading, journaling
1:00–2:30	Three twenty-five-to-thirty-minute periods of centering prayer, first period optional—some participants might choose more unstructured time
2:30–3:00	Reflections on the day

As mentioned above, the centering prayer refresher could consist of a review of the basic guidelines, a brief slide presentation, or a short video. On a quiet day like this you could use centering prayer in its most stripped down form, inviting people into an appropriate posture, setting a timer, ringing a bell to begin the period and again to end it, leaving a couple of minutes of silence after the second bell. Alternatively, you could use the programs in this book to structure at least some of the centering prayer periods into more of a prayer service.

Schedule B	**Day of Centering Prayer and Visio Divina**
10:00–11:00	Introduction to the day Brief centering prayer refresher Very brief introduction to visio divina Questions and comments
11:00–12:15	Two twenty-five-to-thirty-minute periods of centering prayer followed by visio divina
12:15–1:15	Lunch in silence Reflection, discernment, reading, journaling
1:15– 2:30	Two twenty-five-to-thirty-minute periods of centering prayer followed by visio divina
2:30–3:00	Reflections on the day

This schedule is quite similar to Schedule A except that each session of two centering prayer periods leads into a single session of visio divina. This requires that the facilitator say a few words about visio divina at the beginning of the day. If you are going to use the postcard method of visio divina, postcards could be laid out on a table and participants instructed to select one or two as they enter. Another possibility might be to project the visio divina image on a television for the first session and use the postcard method for the second session, inviting participants to select a postcard during the silent lunch. See the chapter "A Concise Guide to Visio Divina" for more ideas.

Sample Discernment Questions for the Handout

- What are the essentials of my spiritual life that will help me to live prayerfully if I do them every day, every week, or every year?
- Is there something that God wants for me that I am not allowing myself that I could make a part of my regular routine?
- Where and when am I most likely to feel the presence of the sacred in my life and how do I make more space for that?
- What is the change I most want to see in the world? What is God's call for me in regard to working for justice and peace?
- What can I do to provide hope, inspiration, and spiritual nourishment to those around me? What can I do to provide practical assistance? Is there a place where these two things intersect in a powerful way?
- What do I most want to bring away with me into my daily life from this day of prayer and reflection? A word of reminder to myself? A feeling? A way of being?

Checklist of Things to Bring

- Singing bowl or chime
- Timer or phone and phone charger
- Clock to see at a glance how you're doing for time
- Basket for donations with sign showing suggested donation amount
- Envelope to put donations into at the end of the day
- Signs to help people find the room where the quiet day is held
- Clipboard to sign up to be on mailing list
- Notes for talks
- Readings
- Books
- Art supplies

- Sharpie, masking tape, and blank pieces of paper, to put up or change room signs, or just in case
- Anything else for special activities

Go with the Flow of the Spirit

Let the Holy Spirit lead the day, blowing where it will. When you are setting a table and inviting participants to bring all parts of themselves, you may include all parts of yourself as well. While as a facilitator you will be focused on holding the space for others, there is also room to be yourself. The emphasis is not on your self-expression, but if the Spirit moves you to be unexpectedly honest, silly, or vulnerable, this may allow the participants to see in you the kind of openness and spontaneity that helps them to go deeper in their practice, their aliveness, and their own listening to the call of the sacred.

At the end of a recent quiet day I asked people what they liked best about the day and several people said that their favorite part was when I couldn't get the slides to project properly on the television in the room and so improvised another solution in a simple, relaxed way. This moment somehow shifted the atmosphere and made it clear that we were in an environment in which we would let go of expectations and gracefully accept whatever was happening. In such moments contemplative practice comes alive.

Describing the spiritual level of consciousness that contemplative prayer helps us access, Thomas Keating writes, "We need to refresh ourselves at this deep level every day. Just as we need exercise, food, rest, and sleep, so also we need moments of interior silence because they bring the deepest kind of refreshment."[xiii] The quiet day is an opportunity to offer to others a more extended taste of this deep refreshment. In silent community participants will experience how our need for rest can take us to the heart of our longing for a deeper relationship with the sacred.

Contemplative Prayer in a Digital Context

PEOPLE WHO ARE DRAWN to silence and contemplative prayer sometimes have a bias against the digital realm, associating it with noise and distraction. Yet the contemplative and digital realms, each a little different from ordinary ways of being in community, can be strangely compatible. In my experience there is deep intimacy to be found using contemplative practices in digital contexts. I find the practice of contemplative prayer in digital community no less moving than in person and many people have expressed the same feeling to me.

I have used the "Program for a Digital Meeting" found in Part III with people all over the world by video conference and telephone conference. Those who find digital groups helpful or even preferable include contemplatives who have trouble finding a local group with which to practice; groups in churches who want to try contemplative prayer but don't have a leader; those who for health, childcare, or other reasons have difficulty leaving their homes; introverts who feel more comfortable meeting from their own homes; those who for various reasons don't want to be physically seen; and busy people who want to avoid travel time. I prefer video conference because it offers the option of seeing each other, but many of the following points apply to the use of telephone conference as well.

Some Points about the Use of Video Conference for Contemplative Practice

Bridges distances—Video eliminates travel times and allows people to connect over great distances and face-to-face at times when they cannot leave their homes or when they are traveling. It can allow geographically isolated or physically challenged people to connect more easily with communities.

Use of silence—Silence experienced with others on digital media can take on a very intentional and powerful quality. When people go to the trouble of being together in silence via digital media, it is clear that the silence is not just an absence of noise.

Safety—Being able to talk from your home, your sofa, even your bed, can give a great feeling of safety. It can also feel quite intimate to be able to give a virtual tour of your home or the view out your window to someone who is far away. Strangers can meet via video without physical safety issues.

Efficient and structured—Meetings via video can facilitate a very structured format, beginning at a quite precise time and eliminating chit chat at the beginning and end of sessions, which can sometimes detract from the spiritual encounter (or sometimes add to it).

Noise—The ambient noise of all the participants on video is aggregated and can be bothersome, more so than on a phone call. This makes video somewhat distracting for long periods of silence and it is often appropriate to use the mute button. However, there can be a certain intimacy to hearing the noises that are taking place in someone else's space.

Shorter meetings—Because participants do not need to travel, it becomes practical to schedule shorter meetings, if desired.

Image—The image can be good for getting to know each other, but there can sometimes be a sense of relief at turning the picture off. Some people prefer not to be seen and this feature is under their control.

Technical difficulties—There can be technical difficulties with getting people on and service cutting out. It's good to leave some extra time to deal with technical issues and not work within a very tight schedule. If you start to feel frustrated, remember how much time you're saving by not having to travel to the meeting.

If someone will be joining a group who has not used video much, it can be helpful to meet with them a few minutes early to make sure they know how to turn their camera on and off, mute themselves, use the chat function and other controls. You may also want to suggest that everyone in the group update their version of the video conferencing software periodically since newer versions may provide better quality reception. If someone can be heard but not seen, this can sometimes be corrected by updating their software.

Latency (sound or picture delays)—Delays can be distracting and are sometimes so severe that communication becomes almost impossible, particularly in areas that do not have high speed internet service. Delays are less likely when using sound only. If the delay is distracting, try ending the call and beginning again or switching to sound only. There is sometimes a delay with the picture coming on at the beginning of the call, particularly with group calls.

Video conferencing technology seems to work best if only one person speaks at a time, with no interruptions. It often does not work well for groups to try to say things in unison because of latency issues. For this reason we usually do not try to chant a psalm together. At the end of a centering prayer group if you are going to say a prayer, some groups may prefer to choose one person to say the prayer as others listen while other groups may prefer the communal spirit of saying the prayer together, even if it sounds a bit chaotic.

Screen sharing—The screen sharing function in Zoom can easily be used to display written prayers, which allows participants to read along. This screen sharing feature can also be used during visio divina to project an image.

Occasionally participants will hit the screen sharing button inadvertently. If the screen suddenly changes unexpectedly you can go to "View Options" and select "Stop Participant's Sharing."

Comparative services and costs—Skype is free to anyone with a computer and a webcam. Some people may resist using Skype at first because they do not realize that it is free and very easy to install. Request that those who will be on the call update their Skype to the latest version by going to the Skype menu—> Check for Updates. Sometimes those who have an older version cannot be seen on the call but can be heard.

I have moved to Zoom for most video meetings. Zoom is free for one-on-one meetings and for groups lasting up to forty minutes and starts at $14.99 per month for unlimited group conferencing. I have found it more reliable and easier to use than Skype. It can easily be used by voice only for those who do not have a camera, participants do not need a Zoom account, and there is less confusion about how to enter a group call or how to record a session. Zoom provides good technical support if you have a problem.

Part III of this book provides a program that may be used for a contemplative prayer group by video conference, simplified in several ways from the regular program. Because of the bounce often experienced in video meetings the digital program begins with a psalm chanted or spoken by the leader alone rather than chanted or read antiphonally by the group. However, since many participants have told me that praying aloud in unison is important to their sense of community I have left the reading of the closing prayer in unison. I have shortened the centering prayer to one period only, partly for simplicity and partly because walking meditation done by individuals in separate locations can be odd and confusing. This simplified program works very well for video conference and can be participated in by those who do not have cameras. The program usually takes about forty to forty-five minutes.

Part III

Programs for Contemplative Prayer Services

Using the Contemplative Prayer Programs

THE CONTEMPLATIVE PRAYER PROGRAMS in this book provide a easy-to-follow model that can be adapted in many ways. A contemplative prayer group could have a number of copies of this book ready for its participants so that they can follow along with a program, just as a church would provide prayer books for services. Alternatively, a group could customize the program and distribute paper copies. Providing participants with either a printed program or a copy of the book when they arrive gives them something informative to look at as they are waiting for the group to begin. You might also invite newcomers to take the printed program home so that they can study it to learn a little bit more about contemplative prayer.

If you choose to create a paper program you can download the text online (see "Resources"). Customize it by inserting the name of your group into the printed program, for example, "Welcome to the Grace Church Brooklyn Heights contemplative prayer group." Add the time of your weekly meeting at the top and your contact information at the bottom. You might also substitute the word "evening" or "morning" for "session" in the welcome section, depending on when your group regularly meets.

Below is a list of the programs you will find in this section. All of them contain the following elements:

- Psalm or choice of psalms
- Welcome

- Invitation to intercessory prayer
- Centering prayer, including instructions for a regular meeting and additional instructions for when beginners are present
- Closing prayer

The following outlines the additional characteristics that distinguish the programs from each other:

- **Program for a Regular Meeting**

Two twenty-minute periods of centering prayer separated by a walking meditation plus simple lectio divina.

- **Program with Visio Divina**

This program differs from the Program for a Regular Meeting only in offering visio divina instead of lectio divina.

- **Program for Home Practice**

While the other three programs are for use in a group, this program is for individual use. It includes a psalm without an antiphon, instructions for one period of centering prayer, and traditional lectio divina.

- **Program for a Digital Meeting**

The program for a meeting by video or teleconference includes a psalm without an antiphon to avoid latency or bounce issues online, and includes only a single period of centering prayer with a simple lectio divina and one choice of closing prayer. The closing prayer may be shown to the group with a screen sharing function by video.

In our experience the regular program with two twenty-minute periods of centering prayer lasts about an hour, while a program with only one period lasts about forty minutes. The Program for Home Practice takes approximately thirty to forty minutes. In all these programs, the following substitutions can easily be made:

- a single period of centering prayer instead of two periods for those who desire a shorter program, or vice versa;
- two thirty-minute periods of centering prayer instead of two twenty-minute periods for those who desire a longer program;
- a brief stretch in place instead of walking meditation, if space is tight or time is short;
- traditional lectio divina instead of simple, or vice versa;
- visio divina instead of lectio divina;
- a different psalm, with or without antiphon;
- a different closing prayer.

Following these four programs is a chapter that outlines four more possible variations :

- Program with Reading and Sharing
- Program with Video and Sharing
- Program with Music
- Program with a Twelve-Step Orientation

Program for a Regular Meeting

This program begins with a choice of two psalms that the group may chant or read together. It provides for two twenty-minute periods of centering prayer separated by a brief walking meditation, but a single twenty- or thirty-minute period may be substituted.

The program offers centering prayer instructions for a regular meeting with additional instructions that may be added if beginners are present. The four basic guidelines of centering prayer are also provided and may be read if beginners are present or if desired. The program continues with a simple lectio divina. The traditional, slightly longer form of lectio divina may be substituted or the lectio divina may be omitted altogether. Two choices of closing prayers are provided. The full program takes approximately an hour; if only one twenty-minute period of centering prayer is substituted, approximately forty minutes.

Before you begin, take a few minutes to choose a brief reading for lectio divina or an alternate psalm and assemble anything else you might need, like a timer or a bell.

Psalm 63, chanted or spoken

Leader	In the shadow of your wings I rejoice, alleluia.
People	*In the shadow of your wings I rejoice, alleluia.*

Leader O God, my God at dawn I seek you,
For you my soul is thirsting,
My flesh is longing,
Like a dry and parched land longs for water.

People *In the shadow of your wings I rejoice, alleluia.*

Leader I have gazed on you in the holy place
To behold your power and your glory.
Better than life itself is your love.
My lips will sing your praise.

People *In the shadow of your wings I rejoice, alleluia.*

Leader I rejoice in the shadow of your wings.
To you my soul has held fast,
You have sustained me by your right hand.

People *In the shadow of your wings I rejoice, alleluia.*

or

Psalm 46, chanted or spoken[xiv]

Leader God whispers to the heart, "Be still; I am with you."

People *God whispers to the heart, "Be still; I am with you."*

Leader God is our refuge and our strength,
a present help in times of trouble.
Therefore we will not fear,
though the earth be moved and shaken.

People *God whispers to the heart, "Be still; I am with you."*

Leader We will not fear
though the mountains be toppled into the sea,
though the depths of the waters rage and foam.

People	*God whispers to the heart, "Be still; I am with you."*
Leader	"Be still, and know that I am God." God is with us, God has spoken, and the earth shall melt away.
People	*God whispers to the heart, "Be still; I am with you."*

Welcome!

Welcome to this contemplative prayer group. This is a place for all God's people. Whatever your beliefs or doubts you are always welcome here. If you are new to centering prayer, just follow the instructions as the session unfolds. You are also welcome to use the silence in any other way that is right for you.

Intercessory Prayer

Leader
Loving God, we ask for your blessings upon this gathering. Recognizing that we bring the joys and sorrows of our lives here, if anyone would like to mention silently or aloud prayers of gratitude or concern for loved ones, the dead or dying, the vulnerable and suffering, or anyone who is facing a special challenge, please do so now.

The people offer prayers, silently or aloud.

Leader
God, we trust that you hear our prayers, silent or spoken, wordless or in words.

Centering Prayer

Leader We begin the first period of centering prayer.

> *Optional instruction for beginners may be added if appropriate:*
>
> We will sit in silence for two twenty-minute periods, separated by a brief walking meditation. I will read the instructions for centering prayer and lead you into the first period. Choose a sacred word as the symbol of your intention to say *yes* to God's transformative presence. Choose any short word with which you are comfortable and that reminds you to be present to God. Examples of a sacred word are Love, Peace, Mercy, Let Go, Silence, God, Amen, Yes.

Continue with regular instructions:

Sit with your back straight and your feet flat on the ground or in another stable position, your hands on your thighs or in your lap. Gently close your eyes. Take a few deep breaths and notice if there are any adjustments you'd like to make to be comfortable for the prayer period. Take a moment to notice who God is for you right now, whatever that might mean, and renew your commitment to be open and present to the divine. Silently begin to repeat the sacred word or touch your breath gently with your attention, using your sacred symbol to orient yourself towards God. During the prayer period, whenever you notice that you have become engaged with your thoughts, gently disengage yourself, returning to the sacred symbol if necessary.

> *The four basic guidelines of centering prayer may be read if beginners are present or on other occasions if desired:*

1. Choose a sacred word or a sacred breath as the symbol of your intention to consent to God's presence and action within.
2. Sitting comfortably and with eyes closed, settle briefly and silently introduce the sacred word or sacred breath as the symbol of your consent to God's presence and action within.
3. When engaged with your thoughts, return ever-so-gently to the sacred word or breath.
4. At the end of the prayer period, remain in silence with eyes closed for a couple of minutes.

Before or just after the leader sets the timer for the first prayer period one of the following short prayers may be said:

- Loving God, deepen our longing for you.
- Loving God, may we rest in your presence.
- We let go of trying to change ourselves,
  and let you, God, arise in our hearts.
- Sacred One, awaken us.

The leader sets the timer for the first prayer period and rings a bell or gong.

> *If beginners are present, at the end of the twenty minute period, as the timer sounds or the leader rings a bell or gong, the leader reads the fourth guideline, followed by a period of silence:*
>
> At the end of the prayer period, remain in silence with eyes closed for a couple of minutes. This is an important transition for bringing the prayer into daily life. If you would like, you can dedicate the period of prayer to a person or concern.

Walking Meditation

Leader Walking meditation.

If beginners are present the leader may add:

As we walk around the room, you can focus on the feeling of your body moving through space or the feeling of your feet touching the floor in order to let go of thoughts and be fully present.

Before or just after the leader sets the timer for the second prayer period one of the following short prayers may be said:

- Loving God, deepen our longing for you.
- Loving God, may we rest in your presence.
- We let go of trying to change ourselves,
  and let you, God, arise in our hearts.
- Sacred One, awaken us.

The leader sets the timer for the second prayer period and rings a bell or gong.

Lectio Divina

Leader
I will read a passage three times, leaving a period of silence after each reading. Listen with the ear of the heart. After the final reading I will invite you to share a word or phrase from the passage that resonated for you.

Reading of the passage, interspersed with silences.

Leader
I invite you to share a word or phrase from the passage that resonated for you.

Closing Prayer

Leader
Let us close by praying together The Prayer of Jesus.

or

Let us close by praying together the Night Prayer.

The Prayer of Jesus

Ground of all being, Mother of life, Father of the universe,
Your name is sacred, beyond speaking.

May we know your presence, may your longings
be our longings in heart and in action.

May there be food for the human family today
and for the whole earth community.

Forgive us the falseness of what we have done
as we forgive those who are untrue to us.

Do not forsake us in our time of conflict
but lead us into new beginnings.

For the light of life, the vitality of life,
and the glory of life are yours now and for ever.

Amen.

—a paraphrase of the Lord's Prayer by John Philip Newell[xv]

Night Prayer

Lord,
it is night.

The night is for stillness.
  Let us be still in the presence of God.

It is night after a long day.
  What has been done has been done;
  what has not been done has not been done;
  let it be.

The night is dark.
  Let our fears of the darkness of the world
  and of our own lives
  rest in you.

The night is quiet.
  Let the quietness of your peace enfold us,
  all dear to us,
  and all who have no peace.

The night heralds the dawn.
  Let us look expectantly to a new day,
  new joys,
  new possibilities.

In your name we pray.
Amen.

—A New Zealand Prayer Book—
He Karakia Mihinare o Aotearoa[xvi]

Program with Visio Divina

This program differs from the regular program only in substituting visio divina for lectio divina. It begins with a choice of two psalms that the group may chant or read together. It provides for two twenty-minute periods of centering prayer separated by a brief walking meditation, but a single twenty- or thirty-minute period may be substituted. The program offers centering prayer instructions for a regular meeting with additional instructions that may be added if beginners are present. The four basic guidelines of centering prayer are also provided and may be read if beginners are present or if desired. The program continues with visio divina. Two choices of closing prayers are provided. The full program takes approximately an hour; if only one twenty-minute period of centering prayer is substituted, approximately forty minutes.

Before you begin, choose the image or images you will use in the visio divina. Suggestions for how to display the images are provided in "A Concise Guide to Visio Divina." Assemble anything else you might need, like a timer, bell, or alternate psalm.

Psalm 63, chanted or spoken

Leader In the shadow of your wings I rejoice, alleluia.

People *In the shadow of your wings I rejoice, alleluia.*

Leader O God, my God at dawn I seek you,
For you my soul is thirsting,
My flesh is longing,
Like a dry and parched land longs for water.

People *In the shadow of your wings I rejoice, alleluia.*

Leader I have gazed on you in the holy place
To behold your power and your glory.
Better than life itself is your love.
My lips will sing your praise.

People *In the shadow of your wings I rejoice, alleluia.*

Leader I rejoice in the shadow of your wings.
To you my soul has held fast,
You have sustained me by your right hand.

People *In the shadow of your wings I rejoice, alleluia.*

or

Psalm 46, chanted or spoken

Leader God whispers to the heart, "Be still; I am with you."

People *God whispers to the heart, "Be still; I am with you."*

Leader God is our refuge and our strength,
a present help in times of trouble.
Therefore we will not fear,
though the earth be moved and shaken.

People *God whispers to the heart, "Be still; I am with you."*

Leader We will not fear
though the mountains be toppled into the sea,
though the depths of the waters rage and foam.

People	*God whispers to the heart, "Be still; I am with you."*
Leader	"Be still, and know that I am God." God is with us, God has spoken, and the earth shall melt away.
People	*God whispers to the heart, "Be still; I am with you."*

Welcome!

Welcome to this contemplative prayer group. This is a place for all God's people. Whatever your beliefs or doubts you are always welcome here. If you are new to centering prayer, just follow the instructions as the session unfolds. You are also welcome to use the silence in any other way that is right for you.

Intercessory Prayer

Leader
Loving God, we ask for your blessings upon this gathering. Recognizing that we bring the joys and sorrows of our lives here, if anyone would like to mention silently or aloud prayers of gratitude or concern for loved ones, the dead or dying, the vulnerable and suffering, or anyone who is facing a special challenge, please do so now.

The people offer prayers, silently or aloud.

Leader
God, we trust that you hear our prayers, silent or spoken, wordless or in words.

Centering Prayer

Leader
We begin the first period of centering prayer.

> *Optional instruction for beginners may be added if appropriate:*
>
> We will sit in silence for two twenty-minute periods, separated by a brief walking meditation. I will read the instructions for centering prayer and lead you into the first period. Choose a sacred word as the symbol of your intention to say *yes* to God's transformative presence. Choose any short word with which you are comfortable and that reminds you to be present to God. Examples of a sacred word are Love, Peace, Mercy, Let Go, Silence, God, Amen, Yes.

Continue with regular instructions:
Sit with your back straight and your feet flat on the ground or in another stable position, your hands on your thighs or in your lap. Gently close your eyes. Take a few deep breaths and notice if there are any adjustments you'd like to make to be comfortable for the prayer period. Take a moment to notice who God is for you right now, whatever that might mean, and renew your commitment to be open and present to the divine. Silently begin to repeat the sacred word or touch your breath gently with your attention, using your sacred symbol to orient yourself towards God. During the prayer period, whenever you notice that you have become engaged with your thoughts, gently disengage yourself, returning to the sacred symbol if necessary.

> *The four basic guidelines of centering prayer may be read if beginners are present or if desired:*
>
> 1. Choose a sacred word or a sacred breath as the symbol of your intention to consent to God's presence and action within.

2. Sitting comfortably and with eyes closed, settle briefly and silently introduce the sacred word or sacred breath as the symbol of your consent to God's presence and action within.
3. When engaged with your thoughts, return ever-so-gently to the sacred word or breath.
4. At the end of the prayer period, remain in silence with eyes closed for a couple of minutes.

Before or just after the leader sets the timer for the first prayer period one of the following short prayers may be said:

- Loving God, deepen our longing for you.
- Loving God, may we rest in your presence.
- We let go of trying to change ourselves,
and let you, God, arise in our hearts.
- Sacred One, awaken us.

The leader sets the timer for the first prayer period and rings a bell or gong.

> *If beginners are present, at the end of the twenty-minute period, as the timer sounds or the leader rings a bell or gong, the leader reads the fourth guideline, followed by a period of silence:*
>
> At the end of the prayer period, remain in silence with eyes closed for a couple of minutes. This is an important transition for bringing the prayer into daily life. If you would like, you can dedicate the period of prayer to a person or concern.

Walking Meditation

Leader Walking meditation.

If beginners are present the leader may add:

As we walk around the room, you can focus on the feeling of your body moving through space or the feeling of your feet touching the floor in order to let go of thoughts and be fully present.

Before or just after the leader sets the timer for the second prayer period one of the following short prayers may be said:

- Loving God, deepen our longing for you.
- Loving God, may we rest in your presence.
- We let go of trying to change ourselves,
  and let you, God, arise in our hearts.
- Sacred One, awaken us.

The leader sets the timer for the second prayer period and rings a bell or gong.

Visio Divina

Leader
Visio divina is a form of divine seeing in which we prayerfully invite God to speak to our hearts as we look at an image. As we gaze together at an image, you will be offered some questions for silent reflection, some of which may speak to you, while others you may choose to ignore. At the end of the visio divina, you will be invited to share a word or phrase to express your experience of the image.

As you gaze at the image, notice your breath and your body.

Pause

Simply be present to the image and allow it to speak to your heart, without any particular agenda. It might speak to you in words or wordlessly.

Pause

How do you feel looking at the image?

Pause

If you had to describe the image in a sentence or two silently to yourself, what would you say?

Pause

If you were in the image, where would you place yourself?

Pause

Do you get a glimpse of the sacred from this image?

Pause

Is God speaking to you in this image?

Pause

Does a name for God arise for you from this image?

Pause

In silence, sit with what you have received.

Pause

Leader
If you choose, I invite you to share aloud a word or phrase to express your experience of the image.

Closing Prayer

Leader
Let us close by praying together the Prayer of Jesus.

or

Let us close by praying together the Night Prayer.

The Prayer of Jesus

Ground of all being, Mother of life, Father of the universe,
Your name is sacred, beyond speaking.

May we know your presence, may your longings
be our longings in heart and in action.

May there be food for the human family today
and for the whole earth community.

Forgive us the falseness of what we have done
as we forgive those who are untrue to us.

Do not forsake us in our time of conflict
but lead us into new beginnings.

For the light of life, the vitality of life,
and the glory of life are yours now and for ever.

Amen.

—a paraphrase of the Lord's Prayer by John Philip Newell[xvii]

Night Prayer

Lord,
it is night.

The night is for stillness.
    Let us be still in the presence of God.

It is night after a long day.
    What has been done has been done;
    what has not been done has not been done;
    let it be.

The night is dark.
    Let our fears of the darkness of the world
    and of our own lives
    rest in you.

The night is quiet.
    Let the quietness of your peace enfold us,
    all dear to us,
    and all who have no peace.

The night heralds the dawn.
    Let us look expectantly to a new day,
    new joys,
    new possibilities.

In your name we pray.
Amen.

—A New Zealand Prayer Book—
He Karakia Mihinare o Aotearoa[xviii]

Program for Home Practice

This program provides some structured suggestions for a home prayer session for those who would like to follow a program very similar to the ones offered for group practice but with language adapted for individual use. Of course, none of these suggestions are necessary for those who would like to pray spontaneously or engage in a simple session of centering prayer. Two choices of psalm are provided. The program includes a twenty- or thirty-minute period of centering prayer and traditional lectio divina, but additional periods of centering prayer may be added and simple lectio divina may be substituted. Two choices of closing prayer are provided. This program takes approximately thirty to forty minutes.

Before you begin, take a few minutes to choose a brief reading for lectio divina or an alternate psalm and assemble anything else you might need, like a timer or a bell.

Psalm, chanted or spoken, silently or aloud

Lord, how beautiful you are;
    how radiant the places you dwell in.
My soul yearns for your presence;
    my whole body longs for your light.
Even the wren finds a house
    and the sparrow a nest for herself.
Take me home, Lord; guide me

to the place of perfect repose.
Let me feel you always within me;
open my eyes to your love.
—from Psalm 84, Stephen Mitchell adaptation[xix]

or

God acts within every moment
and creates the world with each breath,
speaks from the center of the universe,
in the silence beyond all thought.
Mightier than the crash of a thunderstorm,
mightier than the roar of the sea,
is God's voice silently speaking
in the depths of the listening heart.
—Psalm 93, Stephen Mitchell adaptation[xx]

Intercessory Prayer

Loving God, my heart is full of gratitude
for all your blessings.
May I be a vessel of your boundless love
pouring out into the world.
With all my heart and soul
I ask you to hear my prayers and longings.

Offer up prayers silently or aloud. You might keep a list of people and concerns that you would like to pray for, touching each one gently with your attention. Or you might allow prayer concerns to rise up spontaneously during a few minutes of silence.

God, I trust that you hear my prayers
and I ask that I may be part
of your loving movement in the world.

Centering Prayer

If you are new to centering prayer you might take a few moments to review the guidelines before you begin.

Guidelines for Centering Prayer

Choose a sacred word or a sacred breath as the symbol of your intention to consent to God's presence and action within.

Sitting comfortably and with eyes closed, settle briefly and silently introduce the sacred word or breath as the symbol of your consent to God's presence and action within.

When engaged with your thoughts, return ever-so-gently to the sacred word or breath.

Before or just after you set the timer for the prayer period you might say one of the following short prayers:

- Loving God, deepen my longing for you.
- Loving God, may I rest in your presence.
- I let go of trying to change myself,
  and let you, God, arise in my heart.
- Sacred One, awaken me.

Twenty- or thirty-minute period of centering prayer.

At the end of the prayer period, remain in silence with eyes closed for a couple of minutes. This is an important transition for bringing the prayer into daily life.

Lectio Divina

Read the passage through slowly several times, reading with the ear of the heart and leaving plenty of silence in between readings. It can be more powerful to read the passage aloud. If you are struck by a word or phrase as you read, you are welcome to stop and gently repeat it to yourself. Stop at any time just to rest in God's presence. If you choose, each time you read the passage through, keep in mind one of the emphases suggested below:

1. ***Listen** with the ear of the heart. Notice if any phrase, sentence, or word stands out and gently begin to repeat it silently to yourself, allowing it to touch you deeply.*
2. ***Reflect** while you listen to the passage again with deep receptivity. Notice what thoughts, feelings, and reflections arise within you. Let the words resound in your heart. What might God be asking of you through the passage?*
3. ***Respond** spontaneously as you listen. Notice any prayerful response that arises within you, for example a small prayer of gratitude or praise.*
4. ***Rest** in God's presence beyond thoughts or reflections. Just be.*

Closing Prayer

Either The Prayer of Jesus or the Night Prayer.

The Prayer of Jesus

Ground of all being, Mother of life, Father of the universe,
Your name is sacred, beyond speaking.

May we know your presence, may your longings
be our longings in heart and in action.

May there be food for the human family today
and for the whole earth community.

Forgive us the falseness of what we have done
as we forgive those who are untrue to us.

Do not forsake us in our time of conflict
but lead us into new beginnings.

For the light of life, the vitality of life,
and the glory of life are yours now and for ever.

Amen.

—a paraphrase of the Lord's Prayer by John Philip Newell[xxi]

Night Prayer

Lord,
it is night.

The night is for stillness.
    Let us be still in the presence of God.

It is night after a long day.
    What has been done has been done;
    what has not been done has not been done;
    let it be.

The night is dark.
    Let our fears of the darkness of the world
    and of our own lives
    rest in you.

The night is quiet.
    Let the quietness of your peace enfold us,
    all dear to us,
    and all who have no peace.

The night heralds the dawn.
    Let us look expectantly to a new day,
    new joys,
    new possibilities.

In your name we pray.
Amen.

—*A New Zealand Prayer Book—*
He Karakia Mihinare o Aotearoa[xxii]

Program for a Digital Meeting

THIS PROGRAM HAS BEEN ADAPTED for use by video or teleconference. It is recommended that the leader chant or read unaccompanied one of the two psalms provided in order to avoid latency issues. The program allows for one twenty-minute period of centering prayer; two twenty-minute periods or a single thirty-minute period may be substituted for those who desire a longer program. Centering prayer instructions for a regular meeting are offered, with additional instructions that may be added if beginners are present. The program does not include walking meditation; if two periods of centering prayer are used, a simple stretch in between is recommended. The leader may choose to mute all participants during the centering prayer silence.

The program continues with a simple lectio divina. The traditional, slightly longer form of lectio divina or a visio divina may be substituted. Visio divina is a particularly appropriate choice for video use because the screen sharing function makes the image easy to display to all participants. Screen sharing may also be used to display the single closing prayer provided, in which case you may want to type the prayer into a file or photograph it so that it is on your computer ready for display. Alternatively, you could email participants a prayer in advance so that they may read along. The program takes approximately forty minutes; if two twenty-minute periods of centering prayer are substituted, approximately an hour.

Before you begin, take a few minutes to choose a brief reading for lectio divina, an image for visio divina, or an alternate psalm and assemble anything else you might need, like a timer or a bell.

Psalm, Chanted or Spoken by the Leader

Lord, how beautiful you are;
how radiant the places you dwell in.
My soul yearns for your presence;
my whole body longs for your light.
Even the wren finds a house
and the sparrow a nest for herself.
Take me home, Lord; guide me
to the place of perfect repose.
Let me feel you always within me;
open my eyes to your love.
—from Psalm 84, Stephen Mitchell adaptation[xxiii]

or

God acts within every moment
and creates the world with each breath,
speaks from the center of the universe,
in the silence beyond all thought.
Mightier than the crash of a thunderstorm,
mightier than the roar of the sea,
is God's voice silently speaking
in the depths of the listening heart.
—Psalm 93, Stephen Mitchell adaptation[xxiv]

Welcome!

Welcome to this digital contemplative prayer group. This is a place for all God's people. Whatever your beliefs or doubts you are welcome here. If you are new to centering prayer, just follow the instructions as the session unfolds. You are also welcome to use the silence in any other way that is right for you.

Intercessory Prayer

Leader
Loving God, we ask for your blessings upon this gathering. Recognizing that we bring the joys and sorrows of our lives here, if anyone would like to mention silently or aloud prayers of gratitude or concern for loved ones, the dead or dying, the vulnerable and suffering, or anyone who is facing a special challenge, please do so now.

The people offer prayers, silently or aloud.

Leader
God, we trust that you hear our prayers, silent or spoken, wordless or in words.

Centering Prayer

Leader
We begin the first period of centering prayer.

> *Optional instruction for beginners may be added if appropriate:*
>
> We will sit in silence for twenty minutes. I will read the instructions and lead you into the centering prayer. Choose a sacred word as the symbol of your intention to say *yes* to God's transformative presence. Choose any short word with which you are comfortable and that reminds you to be present to God. Examples of a sacred word are Love, Peace, Mercy, Let Go, Silence, God, Amen, Yes.

Continue with regular instructions:

Sit with your back straight and your feet flat on the ground or in another stable position, your hands on your thighs or in your lap. Gently close your eyes. Take a few deep breaths and notice if there are any adjustments you'd like to make to be comfortable for the prayer period. Take a moment to notice who God is for you right now, whatever that might mean, and renew your commitment to be open and present to the divine. Silently begin to repeat the sacred word or touch your breath gently with your attention, using your sacred symbol to orient yourself towards God. During the prayer period, whenever you notice that you have become engaged with your thoughts, gently disengage yourself, returning to the sacred symbol if necessary.

The four basic guidelines of centering prayer may be read if beginners are present or if desired:

1. Choose a sacred word or a sacred breath as the symbol of your intention to consent to God's presence and action within.
2. Sitting comfortably and with eyes closed, settle briefly and silently introduce the sacred word or sacred breath as the symbol of your consent to God's presence and action within.
3. When engaged with your thoughts, return ever-so-gently to the sacred symbol.
4. At the end of the prayer period, remain in silence with eyes closed for a couple of minutes.

Before or just after the leader sets the timer for the prayer period one of the following short prayers may be said:

- Loving God, deepen our longing for you.
- Loving God, may we rest in your presence.
- We let go of trying to change ourselves,
  and let you, God, arise in our hearts.
- Sacred One, awaken us.

The leader sets the timer for the prayer period and rings a bell or gong.

If beginners are present, at the end of the twenty minute period, as the timer sounds or the leader rings a bell or gong, the leader reads the fourth guideline, followed by a period of silence:

At the end of the prayer period, remain in silence with eyes closed for a couple of minutes. This is an important transition for bringing the prayer into daily life. If you would like, you can dedicate the period of prayer to a person or concern.

The timer sounds or the leader rings a bell or gong at the end of the prayer period.

Lectio Divina

Leader
I will read a short passage three times, leaving a period of silence after each reading. Listen with the ear of the heart. At the end I will invite you to share a word or phrase from the passage that resonated for you.

Reading of the passage, interspersed with silences.

Leader
I invite you to share a word or phrase from the passage that resonated for you.

Closing Prayer

Leader
Let us close by praying together The Prayer of Jesus.

If possible, the leader shares his or her screen showing The Prayer of Jesus so that the group may read along.

The Prayer of Jesus

Ground of all being, Mother of life, Father of the universe,
Your name is sacred, beyond speaking.

May we know your presence, may your longings
be our longings in heart and in action.

May there be food for the human family today
and for the whole earth community.

Forgive us the falseness of what we have done
as we forgive those who are untrue to us.

Do not forsake us in our time of conflict
but lead us into new beginnings.

For the light of life, the vitality of life,
and the glory of life are yours now and for ever.

Amen.

—a paraphrase of the Lord's Prayer by John Philip Newell[xxv]

Other Variations on the Program

THE PROGRAM CAN OF COURSE be adapted in many other ways. Would you like to substitute prayers and readings from a different tradition for the psalm and lectio divina reading? Rearrange the activities? Substitute a short stretch-in-place for the walking meditation because your space is too small for walking? Would you prefer a shorter group with only twenty minutes of silent prayer? Or a more talkative group, with time explicitly carved out for sharing afterwards?

Here are outlines for a few more possible variations:

Program with Reading and Sharing

- Psalm
- Welcome
- Intercessory prayer
- Twenty minutes of centering prayer
- Walking meditation
- Reading of a passage from *Open Mind, Open Heart* or another book about contemplative practice, read two or three times with silence in between
- Several minutes of silence
- Sharing—The group members are invited to reflect one at a time on the passage in relation to their contemplative practice

or to their lives. See "Guidelines for Sharing in a Contemplative Group" for ideas on how to structure this.

- Closing prayer

Program with Video and Sharing

- Psalm
- Welcome
- Intercessory prayer
- Twenty minutes of centering prayer
- Walking meditation
- Viewing of a video from the *Six Continuing Sessions* series, see "Resources."
- Sharing—The group members are invited to reflect one at a time on the video in relation to their contemplative practice or to their lives. See "Guidelines for Sharing in a Contemplative Group" for ideas on how to structure this.
- Closing prayer

Program with Music

Short pieces of appropriately contemplative live or recorded music can be interspersed with prayer and silence. For example, one year for each of the six weeks of Lent our group invited a cellist to play the six movements of one of Bach's Cello Suites at various points in our program. The following is an example of a program with three periods of music, but more could be added:

- Music
- Psalm
- Welcome
- Intercessory prayer
- Twenty minutes of centering prayer

- Music
- Simple lectio divina
- Closing prayer
- Music

Program with a Twelve-Step Orientation

Centering prayer can be used by those in twelve-step programs as an eleventh-step practice and is so well suited to this purpose that it may feel like a kind of missing link for those in the twelve-step movement who have been searching for a way to deepen their relationship with God through prayer and meditation. Lectio divina may be used as a method of listening to passages from the *Big Book*. See "Resources" for more information on the 12-Step Outreach service team of Contemplative Outreach and "Readings" for the Serenity Prayer and Prayer of Saint Francis of Assisi. The following is an example of a program that could be used by twelve-step members:

- Serenity Prayer
- Welcome
- Intercessory prayer or third-step prayer
- Twenty minutes of centering prayer
- Reading of a passage from the *Big Book*, read two or three times with silence in between
- Several minutes of silence
- Sharing—The group members are invited to reflect one at a time on the passage in relation to their contemplative practice or to their lives. See "Guidelines for Sharing in a Contemplative Group" for ideas on how to structure this.
- Closing prayer: Prayer of Saint Francis of Assisi

Part IV

Readings and Resources

Readings

Psalms

Unnamable, unthinkable God,
  Lord of the dead and the living,
teach us how transient we are
  and how fragile is everything we love.
For all of us flash into being,
  as insubstantial as a breath.
Our lives are a fleeting shadow;
  then we vanish into the night.

—from Psalm 39, Stephen Mitchell adaptation[xxvi]

Lord, how beautiful you are;
  how radiant the places you dwell in.
My soul yearns for your presence;
  my whole body longs for your light.
Even the wren finds a house
  and the sparrow a nest for herself.
Take me home, Lord; guide me
  to the place of perfect repose.
Let me feel you always within me;
  open my eyes to your love.

—from Psalm 84, Stephen Mitchell adaptation[xxvii]

God acts within every moment
  and creates the world with each breath,
speaks from the center of the universe,
  in the silence beyond all thought.
Mightier than the crash of a thunderstorm,
  mightier than the roar of the sea,
is God's voice silently speaking
  in the depths of the listening heart.

—Psalm 93, Stephen Mitchell adaptation[xxviii]

How long will this pain go on, Lord,
  this grief I can hardly bear?
How long will anguish grip me
  and agony wring my mind?
Light up my eyes with your presence;
  let me feel your love in my bones.
Keep me from losing myself
  in ignorance and despair.
Teach me to be patient, Lord;
  teach me to be endlessly patient.
Let me trust that your love enfolds me
  when my heart feels desolate and dry.
I will sing to the Lord at all times,
  even from the depths of pain.

—Psalm 13, Stephen Mitchell adaptation[xxix]

Even in the midst of great pain, Lord,
  I praise you for that which is.
I will not refuse this grief
  or close myself to this anguish.

Let shallow men pray for ease:
  "Comfort us; shield us from sorrow."
I pray for whatever you send me,
  and I ask to receive it as your gift.
You have put a joy in my heart
  greater than all the world's riches.
I lie down trusting the darkness,
  for I know that even now you are here.

—Psalm 4, Stephen Mitchell adaptation[xxx]

The voice of God is a powerful voice;
  the voice of God is a voice of splendor.
The voice of God breaks the cedar trees;
  God breaks the forest cedars.
The voice of God splits the flames of fire.
  the voice of God shakes the wilderness.
The voice of God makes the oak trees writhe,
  and strips the forest bare.
And in the temple of the Holy One,
  all are crying, "Glory!"

—Psalm 29, adapted from the Saint Helena Psalter[xxxi]

Praise God in the holy places!
  Praise God in the heavenly spheres!
Praise God for mighty works of power!
  Praise God's surpassing greatness!
Praise God with joyful trumpet sound!
  Praise God with lute and harp!
Praise God with dance and laughter!
  Praise God with strings and pipes!

Praise God with resounding cymbals!
  Praise God with crashing cymbals!
Let everything that breathes praise God!
  Praise God, praise God, praise God!

—Psalm 150, Lindsay Boyer adaptation

Loving God, the world is against me today.
I feel the multitudes rising against me
and when I cry out to you I am mocked.
But I feel in your presence an answer,
I cry aloud and your voice rings out to me.
I lie down and sleep, and wake again in your arms.
I am not afraid of the world and its demons.
You rise up, God! You deliver me,
you protect me from the shadows
with your enfolding presence.
You lay a blessing on the one who calls to you.

—Psalm 3, Lindsay Boyer adaptation

Christian Scripture

Now as they went on their way, Jesus entered a certain village, where a woman named Martha welcomed him into her home. She had a sister named Mary, who sat at the Lord's feet and listened to what he was saying. But Martha was distracted by her many tasks; so she came to him and asked, "Lord, do you not care that my sister has left me to do all the work by myself? Tell her then to help me." But the Lord answered her, "Martha, Martha, you are worried and distracted by many things; there is need of only one thing. Mary has chosen the better part, which will not be taken away from her."

Luke 10:38–42

Consider the lilies of the field, clothed in loveliness as they turn their heads toward the sun, trusting that they will receive its rays. Look at the birds of the air, hopping and chirping and flying lightly about; they do not plant or store up their food. Take your place among the trees of the forest; they have greater wisdom than to fret about what to eat or what to wear. The love of God pours down upon us, clothing us and the grass of the field. Like the grass we flourish and then wither, but do not worry about that today.

Matthew 6:25–34, Lindsay Boyer adaptation

When Jesus came to the other side, to the country of the Gadarenes, two demoniacs coming out of the tombs met him. They were so fierce that no one could pass that way. Suddenly they shouted, "What have you to do with us, Son of God? Have you come here to torment us before the time?" Now a large herd of swine was feeding at some distance from them. The demons begged him, "If you cast us out, send us into the herd of swine." And he said to them, "Go!" So they came out and entered the swine; and suddenly, the whole herd rushed down the steep bank into the sea and perished in the water. The swineherds ran off, and on going into the town, they told the whole story about what had happened to the demoniacs. Then the whole town came out to meet Jesus; and when they saw him, they begged him to leave their neighborhood.

—Matthew 8:28–34

Anyone who wants to save his life, must lose it.
Anyone who loses her life will find it.
What gain is there if you win the whole world
  and lose your very self?
What can you offer in exchange for your one life?

—Matthew 16:25–26, Richard Rohr adaptation[xxxii]

When the day of Pentecost had come, the disciples were all together in one place. And suddenly from heaven there came a sound like the rush of a violent wind, and it filled the entire house where they were sitting. Divided tongues, as of fire, appeared among them, and a tongue rested on each of them. All of them were filled with the Holy Spirit and began to speak in other languages, as the Spirit gave them ability. . . . And at this sound the crowd gathered and was bewildered, because each one heard them speaking in the native language of each. Amazed and astonished, they asked, "Are not all these who are speaking Galileans? And how is it that we hear, each of us, in our own native language?" . . . All were amazed and perplexed, saying to one another, "What does this mean?" But others sneered and said, "They are filled with new wine."

—*Acts* 2:1–13

Jesus said therefore, "What is the kingdom of God like? And to what should I compare it? It is like a mustard seed that someone took and sowed in the garden; it grew and became a tree, and the birds of the air made nests in its branches."

And again he said, "To what should I compare the kingdom of God? It is like yeast that a woman took and mixed in with three measures of flour until all of it was leavened."

—*Luke* 13:18–21

Once Jesus was asked by the Pharisees when the kingdom of God was coming, and he answered, "The kingdom of God is not coming with things that can be observed; nor will they say, 'Look, here it is!' or 'There it is!' For, in fact, the kingdom of God is within you."

—*Luke* 17:20–21

Jesus withdrew in a boat to a deserted place by himself. But when the crowds heard it, they followed him on foot from the towns. When he went ashore, he saw a great crowd; and he had compassion for them and cured their sick. When it was evening, the disciples came to him and said, "This is a deserted place, and the hour is now late; send the crowds away so that they may go into the villages and buy food for themselves." Jesus said to them, "They need not go away; you give them something to eat." They replied, "We have nothing here but five loaves and two fish." And he said, "Bring them here to me." Then he ordered the crowds to sit down on the grass. Taking the five loaves and the two fish, he looked up to heaven, and blessed and broke the loaves, and gave them to the disciples, and the disciples gave them to the crowds. And all ate and were filled; and they took up what was left over of the broken pieces, twelve baskets full. And those who ate were about five thousand men, besides women and children.

—Matthew 14:13–21

Jesus called the twelve and began to send them out two by two, and gave them authority over the unclean spirits. He ordered them to take nothing for their journey except a staff; no bread, no bag, no money in their belts; but to wear sandals and not to put on two tunics. He said to them, "Wherever you enter a house, stay there until you leave the place. If any place will not welcome you and they refuse to hear you, as you leave, shake off the dust that is on your feet as a testimony against them." So they went out and proclaimed that all should repent. They cast out many demons, and anointed with oil many who were sick and cured them.

—Mark 6:7–13

As Jesus and his disciples and a large crowd were leaving Jericho, Bartimaeus son of Timaeus, a blind beggar, was sitting by the roadside. When he heard that it was Jesus of Nazareth, he began to shout out and say, "Jesus, Son of David, have mercy on me!" Many sternly ordered him to be quiet, but he cried out even more loudly, "Son of David, have mercy on me!" Jesus stood still and said, "Call him here." And they called the blind man, saying to him, "Take heart; get up, he is calling you." So throwing off his cloak, he sprang up and came to Jesus. Then Jesus said to him, "What do you want me to do for you?" The blind man said to him, "My teacher, let me see again." Jesus said to him, "Go; your faith has made you well." Immediately he regained his sight and followed him on the way.

—*Mark* 10:46–52

Judeo-Christian Scripture

A new heart I will give you, and a new spirit I will put within you; and I will remove from your body the heart of stone and give you a heart of flesh.

—*Ezekiel 36:26*

But Moses said to God, "If I come to the Israelites and say to them, 'The God of your ancestors has sent me to you,' and they ask me, 'What is his name?' what shall I say to them?" God said to Moses, "I AM WHO I AM." He said further, "Thus you shall say to the Israelites, 'I AM has sent me to you.'" God also said to Moses, "Thus you shall say to the Israelites, 'The LORD, the God of your ancestors, the God of Abraham, the God of Isaac, and the God of Jacob, has sent me to you': This is my name forever, and this my title for all generations."

—*Exodus 3:13–15*

Jacob was left alone; and a man wrestled with him until daybreak. When the man saw that he did not prevail against Jacob, he struck him on the hip socket; and Jacob's hip was put out of joint as he wrestled with him. Then he said, "Let me go, for the day is breaking." But Jacob said, "I will not let you go, unless you bless me." So he said to him, "What is your name?" And he said, "Jacob." Then the man said, "You shall no longer be called Jacob, but Israel, for you have striven with God and with humans, and have prevailed." Then Jacob asked him, "Please tell me your name." But he said, "Why is it that you ask my name?" And there he blessed him. So Jacob called the place Peniel, saying, "For I have seen God face to face, and yet my life is preserved."

—*Genesis 32: 24–30*

Moses was keeping the flock of his father-in-law Jethro, the priest of Midian; he led his flock beyond the wilderness, and came to Horeb, the mountain of God. There the angel of the LORD appeared to him in a flame of fire out of a bush; he looked, and the bush was blazing, yet it was not consumed. Then Moses said, "I must turn aside and look at this great sight, and see why the bush is not burned up." When the LORD saw that he had turned aside to see, God called to him out of the bush, "Moses, Moses!" And he said, "Here I am." Then he said, "Come no closer! Remove the sandals from your feet, for the place on which you are standing is holy ground." He said further, "I am the God of your father, the God of Abraham, the God of Isaac, and the God of Jacob." And Moses hid his face, for he was afraid to look at God.

—*Exodus 3:1–6*

Poems

The Guest House

This being human is a guest house.
Every morning a new arrival.

A joy, a depression, a meanness,
some momentary awareness comes
as an unexpected visitor.

Welcome and entertain them all!
Even if they're a crowd of sorrows,
who violently sweep your house
empty of its furniture,
still, treat each guest honorably.
He may be clearing you out
for some new delight.

The dark thought, the shame, the malice,
meet them at the door laughing,
and invite them in.

Be grateful for whoever comes,
because each has been sent
as a guide from beyond.

—*Jelaluddin Rumi*[xxxiii]

Lo, I am with you always means when you look for God,
God is in the look of your eyes,
in the thought of looking, nearer to you than your self,
or things that have happened to you.
There's no need to go outside.

Be melting snow.
Wash yourself of yourself.

A white flower grows in the quietness.
Let your tongue become that flower.

—*Jelaluddin Rumi*[xxxiv]

God speaks to each of us as he makes us,
then walks with us silently out of the night.

These are the words we dimly hear:

You, sent out beyond your recall,
go to the limits of your longing.
Embody me.

Flare up like flame
and make big shadows I can move in.

Let everything happen to you: beauty and terror.
Just keep going. No feeling is final.
Don't let yourself lose me.

Nearby is the country they call life.
You will know it by its seriousness.

Give me your hand.

—*Rainer Maria Rilke*[xxxv]

Cover Me with the Night

Come, Lord,
and cover me with the night.
Spread your grace over us
as you assured us you would do.

Your promises are more than
all the stars in the sky;
your mercy is deeper than the night.
Lord, it will be cold.
The night comes with its breath of death.
Night comes; the end comes; you come.

Lord, we wait for you
day and night.

—*A Prayer from Ghana*[xxxvi]

The Peace of Wild Things

When despair for the world grows in me
and I wake in the night at the least sound
in fear of what my life and my children's lives may be,
I go and lie down where the wood drake
rests in his beauty on the water, and the great heron feeds.
I come into the peace of wild things
who do not tax their lives with forethought
of grief. I come into the presence of still water.
And I feel above me the day-blind stars
waiting with their light. For a time
I rest in the grace of the world, and am free.

—*Wendell Berry*[xxxvii]

Primary Wonder

Days pass when I forget the mystery.
Problems insoluble and problems offering
their own ignored solutions
jostle for my attention, they crowd its antechamber
along with a host of diversions, my courtiers, wearing
their colored clothes; caps and bells.
And then
once more the quiet mystery
is present to me, the throng's clamor
recedes: the mystery
that there is anything, anything at all,
let alone cosmos, joy, memory, everything,
rather than void: and that, O Lord,
Creator, Hallowed one, You still,
hour by hour sustain it.

—*Denise Levertov*[xxxviii]

Go in and in.
  Be the space
between two cells,
  the vast, resounding
silence in which
  spirit dwells.
Be sugar dissolving
  on the tongue of life.
Dive in and in,
  as deep as you can dive.
Be infinite, ecstatic truth.
  Be love conceived and born in union.
Be exactly what you seek,
  the Beloved, singing Yes,
tasting Yes, embracing Yes
  until there is only essence;
the All of Everything
  expressing through you
as you. Go in and in
  and turn away from
nothing that you find.

—Danna Faulds[xxxix]

Spiritual Classics

Abbot Lot came to Abbot Joseph and said: Father, according as I am able, I keep my little rule, and my little fast, my prayer, meditation, and contemplative silence; and according as I am able I strive to cleanse my heart of thoughts: now what more should I do? The elder rose up in reply and stretched out his hands to heaven, and his fingers became like ten lamps of fire. He said: Why not be totally changed into fire?

—*The Desert Fathers and Mothers*[xl]

My Lord God, I have no idea where I am going. I do not see the road ahead of me. I cannot know for certain where it will end. Nor do I really know myself, and the fact that I think I am following your will does not mean that I am actually doing so. But I believe that the desire to please you does in fact please you. And I hope I have that desire in all that I am doing. I hope that I will never do anything apart from that desire. And I know that if I do this you will lead me by the right road, though I may know nothing about it. Therefore I will trust you always, though I may seem to be lost and in the shadow of death. I will not fear, for you are ever with me, and you will never leave me to face my perils alone.

—*Thomas Merton*[xli]

We awaken in Christ's body,
As Christ awakens our bodies
There I look down and my poor hand is Christ,
He enters my foot and is infinitely me.
I move my hand and wonderfully
My hand becomes Christ,
Becomes all of Him.
I move my foot and at once
He appears in a flash of lightning.
Do my words seem blasphemous to you?
—Then open your heart to Him.
And let yourself receive the One
Who is opening to you so deeply.
For if we genuinely love Him,
We wake up inside Christ's body
Where all our body all over,
Every most hidden part of it,
Is realized in joy as Him,
And He makes us utterly real.
And everything that is hurt, everything
That seemed to us dark, harsh, shameful,
maimed, ugly, irreparably damaged
Is in Him transformed.
And in Him, recognized as whole, as lovely,
And radiant in His light,
We awaken as the beloved
In every last part of our body.

—Symeon the New Theologian[xlii]

Spiritual Writing

You are accepted.
You are accepted,
accepted by that which is greater than you,
and the name of which you do not know.
Do not ask for the name now; perhaps you will find it later.
Do not try to do anything now; perhaps later you will do much.
Do not seek for anything; do not perform anything;
do not intend anything.
Simply accept the fact that you are accepted!
If that happens to us, we experience grace.

—Paul Tillich[xliii]

Vocation does not come from willfulness. It comes from listening. I must listen to my life and try to understand what it is truly about—quite apart from what I would like it to be about—or my life will never represent anything real in the world, no matter how earnest my intentions. That insight is hidden in the word *vocation* itself, which is rooted in the Latin for "voice." Vocation does not mean a goal that I pursue. It means a calling that I hear. Before I can tell my life what I want to do with it, I must listen to my life telling me who I am. I must listen for the truths and values at the heart of my own identity, not the standards by which I *must* live—but the standards by which I cannot help but live if I am living my own life.

—Parker J. Palmer[xliv]

Contemplative prayer is the world in which God can do anything. To move into that realm is the greatest adventure. It is to be open to the Infinite and hence to infinite possibilities. Our private, self-made worlds come to an end; a new world appears within and around us and the impossible becomes an everyday experience.

—*Thomas Keating*[xlv]

Interior silence is one of the most strengthening and affirming of human experiences. There is nothing more affirming, in fact, than the experience of God's presence and love. That revelation says as nothing else can, "You are a good person. I created you and I love you." Divine love brings us into being in the fullest sense of the word. It heals the negative feelings we have about ourselves.

—*Thomas Keating*[xlvi]

Twelve-Step Tradition

The Serenity Prayer

God grant me the serenity
to accept the things I cannot change,
courage to change the things I can,
and the wisdom to know the difference.

—Reinhold Niebuhr

Prayer of Saint Francis of Assisi

Lord, make me an instrument of your peace.
Where there is hatred, let me bring love.
Where there is offense, let me bring pardon.
Where there is discord, let me bring union.
Where there is error, let me bring truth.
Where there is doubt, let me bring faith.
Where there is despair, let me bring hope.
Where there is darkness, let me bring your light.
Where there is sadness, let me bring joy.
O Master, let me not seek as much
to be consoled as to console,
to be understood as to understand,
to be loved as to love,
for it is in giving that we receive,
it is in self-forgetting that we find,
it is in pardoning that we are pardoned,
it is in dying that we are born to eternal life.

Buddhist Writing

Our true home is in the present moment. The miracle is not to walk on water. The miracle is to walk on the green earth in the present moment. Peace is all around us—in the world and in nature—and within us—in our bodies and our spirits. Once we learn to touch this peace, we will be healed and transformed. It is not a matter of faith; it is a matter of practice. We need only to bring our body and mind into the present moment, and we will touch what is refreshing, healing, and wondrous.

—*Thich Nhat Hanh*[xlvii]

Let me respectfully
remind you,
life and death
are of supreme importance.
Time swiftly passes by
and opportunity is lost.
Each of us should strive to awaken.
Awaken. Take heed.
Do not squander your life.

—*Evening Gatha*[xlviii]

Things falling apart is a kind of testing and also a kind of healing. We think that the point is to pass the test or to overcome the problem, but the truth is that things don't really get solved. They come together and they fall apart. Then they come together again and fall apart again. It's just like that. The healing comes from letting there be room for all of this to happen: room for grief, for relief, for misery, for joy.

—*Pema Chödrön*[xlix]

The great gift of a spiritual path is coming to trust that you can find a way to true refuge. You realize that you can start right where you are, in the midst of your life, and find peace in any circumstance. Even at those moments when the ground shakes terribly beneath you—when there's a loss that will alter your life forever—you can still trust that you will find your way home. This is possible because you've touched the timeless love and awareness that are intrinsic to who you are.

—*Tara Brach*[l]

When we let go of our battles and open our heart to things as they are, then we come to rest in the present moment. This is the beginning and the end of spiritual practice. Only in this moment can we discover that which is timeless. Only here can we find the love that we seek. Love in the past is simply memory, and love in the future is fantasy. Only in the reality of the present can we love, can we awaken, can we find peace and understanding and connection with ourselves and the world.

—*Jack Kornfield*[li]

Resources

DOWNLOADABLE CONTEMPLATIVE PRAYER PROGRAMS from this book, recordings of chanted psalms, as well as additional materials on contemplative prayer and news about upcoming events are available on **my website Spirituality for Questioning Minds at lindsayboyer.com.**

Centering Prayer

Thomas Keating, *Open Mind, Open Heart* (New York: Continuum, 2008)
This classic book by one of the founders and great exponents of centering prayer is one of the most influential books on this subject. Much of the book is in a practical question-and-answer format.

David Frenette, *The Path of Centering Prayer: Deepening Your Experience of God* (Boulder, CO: Sounds True, 2012)
David Frenette has taught centering prayer under Thomas Keating's guidance since 1984 and is my own teacher. This wonderful book provides a good introduction for beginners but also goes more deeply into the practice for the more experienced practitioner. It contains detailed instruction for those who would like to use the sacred breath.

Cynthia Bourgeault, *Centering Prayer and Inner Awakening* (Cambridge, MA: Cowley, 2004)

Episcopal priest and gifted teacher Cynthia Bourgeault has worked closely with centering prayer founder Thomas Keating. This book is an excellent guide for those who would like to go deeper into centering prayer. It includes a good chapter on the welcoming prayer.

Contemplative Outreach Website, contemplativeoutreach.org
Contemplative Outreach is the international organization responsible for spreading centering prayer throughout the world. Their website is a great resource for learning about weekly centering prayer groups in your area, retreats, courses, and other centering prayer resources.

Centering Prayer Mobile App
This free app includes an adjustable timer, opening and closing prayer options that may be read before and after centering prayer, an assortment of bell sounds, and brief instructions for centering prayer.

Lectio Divina

Thelma Hall, *Too Deep for Words: Rediscovering Lectio Divina* (Mahwah, NJ: Paulist, 1988)
This classic book contains not only instruction and theological background for traditional lectio divina but many reference numbers for scripture passages that may be used in lectio divina.

Christine Valters Paintner, *Lectio Divina—The Sacred Art: Transforming Words and Images into Heart-Centered Prayer* (Woodstock, VT: Skylight Paths, 2012)
This book approaches lectio divina with openness and creativity, exploring traditional and non-traditional approaches. Includes passages and questions for reflection.

Walking Meditation

Thich Nhat Hanh, *How to Walk* (Berkeley: Parallax, 2015)
This small book collects some of the writings of the Vietnamese monk and peace activist Thich Nhat Hanh, a master of walking meditation, and gives a great sense of the flavor of the practice.

Chanting and the Psalms

Cynthia Bourgeault, *Chanting the Psalms: A Practical Guide with Instructional CD* (Boston: New Seeds, 2006)
An introduction to chanting the Psalms, from the simplest monotone to more complex systems, including a CD that provides examples of all the different styles. Chanting is a wonderful practice for those who are looking for a more embodied form of prayer.

The Psalms

***The Saint Helena Psalter* (New York: Church, 2004)**
The sisters of the Order of St. Helena have created a lovely version of the Psalms that features fully inclusive language while remaining close to the traditional language of *The Book of Common Prayer*.

Stephen Mitchell, *A Book of Psalms: Selected and Adapted from the Hebrew* (New York: HarperCollins, 1993)
A selection of the Psalms, translated quite loosely and very beautifully by the well-known translator and poet.

Nan Merrill, *Psalms for Praying: An Invitation to Wholeness* (New York: Continuum, 2004)
Merrill has reworked the Psalms with gentle, loving language, leaving out mentions of anger and vengeance.

Christian Contemplative Prayer in Context

Thomas Keating, *Invitation to Love: The Way of Christian Contemplation* (London: Bloomsbury, 2012)
This book by one of the founders and great exponents of centering prayer explores the spiritual growth that takes place when centering prayer is seriously undertaken.

Cynthia Bourgeault, *The Wisdom Jesus: Transforming Heart and Mind—A New Perspective on Christ and His Message* (Boston: Shambhala, 2008)
Episcopal priest and gifted teacher Cynthia Bourgeault traces contemplative teaching back to Jesus's words and explores with depth and insight how Jesus invites us into a transformation of consciousness.

Richard Rohr, *The Naked Now: Learning to See as the Mystics See* (New York: Crossroad, 2009)
This exploration of the teachings of Jesus and the Christian mystics by the Franciscan priest and great teacher Richard Rohr makes clear why contemplative practice is essential: "We must move from a belief-based religion to a practice-based religion, or little will change."

Further Sources for Readings

Stephen Mitchell, *The Enlightened Heart: An Anthology of Sacred Poetry* (New York: Harper Perennial, 1993) and *The Enlightened Mind: An Anthology of Sacred Prose* (New York: HarperCollins, 1991)
These two anthologies of sacred poetry and prose from the world's great religious and literary traditions are chockablock with beautiful readings. *The Enlightened Heart* in particular is a common source of readings in our group.

***The Daily Reader for Contemplative Living: Excerpts from the Works of Father Thomas Keating,* compiled by S. Stephanie Iachetta (New York: Continuum, 2007)**
Short selections from the writings of Thomas Keating on centering prayer and contemplative aspects of the spiritual life.

Anita Barrows and Joanna Macy, *Rilke's Book of Hours: Love Poems to God* (New York: Riverhead, 2005)
Beautifully translated sacred poems by the great Rainer Maria Rilke.

Stephen Mitchell, *Tao Te Ching: A New English Version* (New York: Harper Perennial, 1988)
Poet Mitchell's luminous translation of the Taoist classic is a great source of readings for interfaith events.

Rumi, *The Essential Rumi*, translated by Coleman Barks with John Moyne (New York: HarperCollins, 1995)
Poet Robert Bly gave Coleman Barks an academic translation of Rumi with the words "these poems need to be released from their cages." Thus began Barks's more than thirty-year project of freely adapting the thirteenth-century Persian poet's ecstatic verses into new and inspiring forms.

Mary Oliver, *New and Selected Poems* (Boston: Beacon, 1992)
Oliver's acute observations of the natural world from her daily walks resulted in classic poems such as "Wild Geese" and "The Summer Day."

The Lectionary Page at lectionarypage.net
The Lectionary provides weekly and sometimes daily verses of scripture that will be read in church that week for those who would like to coordinate their lectio divina readings with the church calendar. Readings are often a bit long for lectio divina but may be abridged.

Group Dynamics

Parker Palmer, *A Hidden Wholeness: The Journey Towards an Undivided Life* (San Francisco: Jossey-Bass, 2004)
For those who would like to go deeper in exploring how to create safe and sacred space in groups, Palmer builds on his experience of the Quaker tradition to illustrate how we can listen to and support each other in community through the use of open, honest questions, creating circles of trust.

Online Resources

Spirituality for Questioning Minds at lindsayboyer.com
Downloadable contemplative prayer programs from this book, recordings of chanted psalms as well as additional materials on contemplative prayer and news about upcoming events are available on my website.

Contemplative Outreach at contemplativeoutreach.org
Contemplative Outreach is a spiritual network of individuals and small faith communities committed to living the contemplative dimension of the gospel. Their website is a great source of information about centering prayer and other contemplative prayer groups, centering prayer introductions, retreats, online groups, and videos.

12-Step Outreach at cp12stepoutreach.org
Centering prayer can be used by those in twelve-step programs as an eleventh-step practice and is so well suited to this purpose that it may feel like a kind of missing link for those in the twelve-step movement who have been searching for a way to deepen their relationship with God through prayer and meditation. Contemplative Outreach has developed a number of ways of offering centering prayer to people in twelve-step fellowships. The 12-Step Outreach website offers numerous resources on centering prayer as an eleventh step practice.

Richard Rohr's Daily Email Meditations at cac.org/sign-up/
I begin my day with Richard Rohr's short, free, daily email reflections on contemplative spirituality. A Franciscan monk, Rohr has a deep appreciation of the spirituality of other religions and is very good at discussing with sensitivity and balance the ways in which Christians have gone off course and suggesting how Christian scripture and theology can be interpreted with intelligence, tolerance, simplicity, and love.

Six Continuing Sessions of the Introduction to the Centering Prayer Practice at https://youtu.be/W4w52bsLGrw
This series of six half-hour videos by Thomas Keating makes a great introduction to centering prayer and could be used as the basis for a video discussion group.

Endnotes

i. Rumi, *The Essential Rumi*, 51.

ii. Merrill, *Lumen Christi . . . Holy Wisdom*, 48.

iii. Teresa of Avila, quoted in Keating, *Fruits and Gifts*, 1.

iv. Tillich, *The Essential Paul Tillich*, 201.

v. Keating, *Invitation to Love,* 105.

vi. Keating, *Open Mind, Open Heart,* 35.

vii. Bourgeault, *Centering Prayer and Inner Awakening*, 23–24.

viii. Frenette, *Path of Centering Prayer*, 18–21.

ix. Frenette, *Path of Centering Prayer,* 77.

x. Fitzpatrick-Hopler, "The Practice of Visio Divina," 2.

xi. Nhat Hanh, *How to Walk*, 8, 21.

xii. Order of Saint Helena, *Saint Helena Psalter*, 168.

xiii. Keating, *Open Mind, Open Heart,* 20.

xiv. I am indebted to liturgist Judy Burns for the adaptation of the antiphon of this psalm.

xv. Reprinted with permission from Newell, *Sounds of the Eternal*, 86.

xvi. Reprinted with permission from Anglican Church in New Zealand. *A New Zealand Prayer Book—He Karakia Mihinare o Aotearoa*, 184.

xvii. Reprinted with permission from Newell, *Sounds of the Eternal*, 86.

xviii. Reprinted with permission from Anglican Church in New Zealand. *A New Zealand Prayer Book—He Karakia Mihinare o Aotearoa*, 184.

xix. Mitchell, *A Book of Psalms*, 37.

xx. Mitchell, *A Book of Psalms*, 42, with one word changed by permission of the author.

xxi. Reprinted with permission from Newell, *Sounds of the Eternal*, 86.

xxii. Reprinted with permission from Anglican Church in New Zealand. *A New Zealand Prayer Book—He Karakia Mihinare o Aotearoa*, 184.

xxiii. Mitchell, *A Book of Psalms*, 37.

xxiv. Mitchell, *A Book of Psalms*, 42, with one word changed by permission of the author.

xxv. Reprinted with permission from Newell, *Sounds of the Eternal*, 86.

xxvi. Mitchell, *A Book of Psalms*, 22.

xxvii. Mitchell, *A Book of Psalms*, 37.

xxviii. Mitchell, *A Book of Psalms*, 42, with one word changed by permission of the author.

xxix. Mitchell, *A Book of Psalms*, 6.

xxx. Mitchell, *A Book of Psalms*, 4.

xxxi. Order of Saint Helena, *Saint Helena Psalter*, 39.

xxxii. Matt 16:25–26, Rohr adaptation from *Falling Upwards*, 73.

xxxiii. Rumi, *The Essential Rumi*, 109.

xxxiv. Rumi, *The Essential Rumi*, 13.

xxxv. Rilke, *Rilke's Book of Hours*, 119.

xxxvi. Tutu, *An African Prayer Book*, 122.

xxxvii. Berry, *Selected Poems of Wendell Berry*, 30.

xxxviii. Levertov, *Sands of the Well*, 129.

xxxix. Faulds, *Go In and In*, 2.

xl. Merton, *Wisdom of the Desert*, 50.

xli. Merton, *Thoughts in Solitude*, 79.

xlii. Symeon the New Theologian, "Hymn 15," *Hymns of Divine Love*, adaptation from Rohr, *Things Hidden*, 218–19.

xliii. Tillich, *The Essential Paul Tillich*, 201.

xliv. Palmer, *Let Your Life Speak*, 4.

xlv. Keating, *Open Mind, Open Heart*, 11.

xlvi. Keating, *Open Mind, Open Heart*, 60.

xlvii. Nhat Hanh, *Living Buddha, Living Christ*, 23–24.

xlviii. Loori, *Zen Mountain Monastery Liturgy Manual*, 47.

xlix. Chödrön, *When Things Fall Apart*, 10.

l. Brach, *True Refuge*, 45.

li. Kornfield, *A Path with Heart*, 26.

Bibliography

Anglican Church in Aotearoa, New Zealand and Polynesia—Te Haahi Mihanare ki Aotearoa ki Niu Tireni, ki Nga Moutere o te Moana Nui a Kiwa. *A New Zealand Prayer Book—He Karakia Mihinare o Aotearoa*. San Francisco: Harper SanFrancisco, 1997.

Berry, Wendell. "The Peace of Wild Things." In *The Selected Poems of Wendell Berry*, 30. Berkeley: Counterpoint, 2009.

Bourgeault, Cynthia. *Centering Prayer and Inner Awakening*. Cambridge, MA: Cowley, 2004.

Brach, Tara. *True Refuge: Finding Peace and Freedom in Your Own Awakened Heart*. New York: Bantam, 2013.

Chödrön, Pema. *When Things Fall Apart: Heart Advice for Difficult Times*. Boston: Shambhala, 2005.

Faulds, Danna. *Go In and In: Poems from the Heart of Yoga*. Kearney, NE: Morris, 2002.

Fitzpatrick-Hopler, Gail. "The Practice of Visio Divina: Seeing with the Eye of the Heart." *Contemplative Outreach News*, June 2015, https://www.contemplativeoutreach.org/sites/default/files/newsletter-pdf/2015-june-newsletter.pdf

Frenette, David. *The Path of Centering Prayer: Deepening Your Experience of God*. Boulder, CO: Sounds True, 2012.

Keating, Thomas. *Fruits and Gifts of the Spirit*. Herndon, VA: Lantern, 2000.

———. *Invitation to Love: The Way of Christian Contemplation*. London: Bloomsbury, 2012.

———. *Open Mind, Open Heart: 20th Anniversary Edition*. New York: Continuum, 2008.

Kornfield, Jack. *A Path with Heart: A Path through the Perils and Promises of Spiritual Life*. New York: Bantam, 1993.

Levertov, Denise. "Primary Wonder." In *Sands of the Well*, 129. New York: New Directions, 1996.

Loori, John Daido, ed. *Zen Mountain Monastery Liturgy Manual*. Mt. Tremper, NY: Dharma, 1998.

Merrill, Nan C. *Lumen Christi . . . Holy Wisdom: Journey to Awakening*. New York: Continuum, 2002.

Merton, Thomas. "Some Sayings of the Desert Fathers." In *Wisdom of the Desert*, 50. New York: New Directions, 1960.

———. *Thoughts in Solitude*. New York: Farrar, Straus and Giroux, 1958.

Mitchell, Stephen. *A Book of Psalms: Selected and Adapted from the Hebrew*. New York: HarperCollins, 1993.

National Council of the Churches of Christ in the U.S.A. *New Revised Standard Version Bible*. New York: Oxford University Press, 1989.

Newell, John Philip. *Sounds of the Eternal: A Celtic Psalter*. San Antonio, TX: Material Media, 2012.

Nhat Hanh, Thich. *How to Walk*. Berkeley: Parallax, 2015.

———. *Living Buddha, Living Christ*. New York: Riverhead, 1995.

Order of Saint Helena. *The Saint Helena Psalter*. New York: Church, 2004.

Palmer, Parker J. *Let Your Life Speak: Listening for the Voice of Vocation*. San Francisco: Jossey-Bass, 2000.

Rilke, Rainer Maria. *Rilke's Book of Hours: Love Poems to God*. Translated by Anita Barrows and Joanna Macy. New York: Riverhead, 2005.

Rohr, Richard. *Falling Upwards: A Spirituality for the Two Halves of Life*. San Francisco: Jossey-Bass, 2013.

———. *Things Hidden: Scripture As Spirituality*. Cincinnati, OH: St. Anthony Messenger, 2008.

Rumi. "An Empty Garlic," "The Guest House," and "Be Melting Snow." In *The Essential Rumi*, translated by Coleman Barks with John Moyne, 51, 109, 13. New York: HarperCollins, 1995.

Tillich, Paul. "You Are Accepted." In *The Essential Paul Tillich: An Anthology of the Writings of Paul Tillich,* edited by F. Forrester Church, 194–204. Chicago: University of Chicago Press, 1987.

Tutu, Desmond. "Cover Me with the Night." In *An African Prayer Book*, 122. New York: Doubleday, 1995.

Subject Index

Scripture Index

Made in the USA
Las Vegas, NV
16 October 2021